# Policy Framework on Sound Public Governance

## BASELINE FEATURES OF GOVERNMENTS THAT WORK WELL

**OECD))**

BETTER POLICIES FOR BETTER LIVES

This document, as well as any data and map included herein, are without prejudice to the status of or sovereignty over any territory, to the delimitation of international frontiers and boundaries and to the name of any territory, city or area.

The statistical data for Israel are supplied by and under the responsibility of the relevant Israeli authorities. The use of such data by the OECD is without prejudice to the status of the Golan Heights, East Jerusalem and Israeli settlements in the West Bank under the terms of international law.

Note by Turkey
The information in this document with reference to "Cyprus" relates to the southern part of the Island. There is no single authority representing both Turkish and Greek Cypriot people on the Island. Turkey recognises the Turkish Republic of Northern Cyprus (TRNC). Until a lasting and equitable solution is found within the context of the United Nations, Turkey shall preserve its position concerning the "Cyprus issue".

Note by all the European Union Member States of the OECD and the European Union
The Republic of Cyprus is recognised by all members of the United Nations with the exception of Turkey. The information in this document relates to the area under the effective control of the Government of the Republic of Cyprus.

**Please cite this publication as:**
OECD (2020), *Policy Framework on Sound Public Governance: Baseline Features of Governments that Work Well*, OECD Publishing, Paris, *https://doi.org/10.1787/c03e01b3-en*.


ISBN 978-92-64-56478-7 (print)
ISBN 978-92-64-55578-5 (pdf)

# Foreword

Governments face increasingly multidimensional policy challenges in conjunction with scarce public resources and low levels of trust in government. The 2008 financial crisis, and more recently the COVID-19 pandemic, have highlighted this state of affairs in the starkest possible terms. Traditional analytical tools and approaches are no longer fit for purpose in the current environment. Classic governance problems, often caused by the inadequate design or poor management of institutions, are exacerbating the need to adapt to rapid political and technological developments. The challenges of our time therefore require a crosscutting, integrated and innovative governance approach. More than ever, governments and citizens need public institutions that can anticipate difficult policy issues and respond to them coherently and effectively, in the public interest. The OECD strives to support this endeavour by gathering evidence and creating legal instruments that promote principles and good practices across key thematic areas of public governance.

Weaving together existing OECD legal standards in public governance and lessons learned over the course of the past decade, the Policy Framework on Sound Public Governance aggregates baseline features found in governments that work well. Acknowledging that each government possesses unique strengths and areas for improvement, this Framework provides governments with an integrated baseline diagnostic, guidance and benchmarking tool to design and implement governance reforms. It reflects a broad consultation process with OECD members, international organisations, civil society organisations and the public.

The Framework posits that effective democratic institutions lie at the core of pluralist democracies and are indispensable not only for reform, but, more importantly, for engaging in open, equitable and inclusive decision-making in the public interest, with the ultimate goal of enhancing wellbeing and prosperity for all. As defined in the Framework, sound public governance is a combination of three interconnected and largely mutually dependent elements: values, enablers, and instruments and tools. The key governance values presented in the Framework underpin the way in which governments select and prioritise policy problems, take policy decisions and structure their relations with stakeholders. The Framework then identifies a nexus of enablers that support government pursuing effective and equitable decision-making and reform. Finally, sound public governance also directly relates to how governments formulate, implement, communicate and evaluate reforms and policies. To this end, the Framework presents the policy instruments and management tools used by governments at different stages of the policy cycle to shape these core components of policy-making.

With this Framework, the OECD offers governments guidance for ensuring that their core institutional and decision-making arrangements are suited to the contemporary policy landscape and lead to better outcomes for people.

# Acknowledgements

The *Policy Framework on Sound Public Governance* was developed by a team led by Adam Knelman Ostry, Head of the Public Governance Reviews Unit in the Governance Reviews and Partnerships Division (GRP) of the OECD Public Governance Directorate (GOV), and project manager of this work. It was prepared under the guidance of Martin Forst, Head of GRP and Janos Bertok, Acting Director of GOV. Mr Ostry provided strategic guidance to the Framework's co-ordinators and principal drafters, Iván Stola and Johannes Klein, and to its researcher Emma Phillips. Communications advice was provided by Roxana Glavanov, Amelia Godber and Justin Kavanagh. Editorial support was provided by Patricia Marcelino, and production support by Raquel Paramo. Caroline Varley initiated in 2013 the assessment of lessons learned from a decade's worth of OECD Public Governance Reviews, from which this Policy Framework draws much of its evidence. Rolf Alter, GOV Director until 2017, provided initial strategic leadership for this work.

This Policy Framework reflects a collective effort with contributions from across the Public Governance Directorate, including from Daniel Acquah, Moritz Ader, Julio Bacio Terracino, Karine Badr, Alessandro Bellantoni, Pauline Bertrand, Eva Beuselinck, Emma Cantera, Marco Daglio, Andrew Davies, Ebba Dohlman, Sara Fyson, Daniel Gerson, David Goessmann, Pinar Guven, Stephane Jacobzone, Céline Kauffmann, Edwin Lau, Chloé Lelievre, Carina Lindberg, Craig Matasick, Cristina Mendes, Carissa Munro, Mariana Prats, Alex Roberts, Ana Maria Ruiz Rivadaneira, Claire Salama, Ernesto Soria Morales, Tatyana Teplova, Daniel Trnka, Bagrat Tunyan, Barbara Ubaldi, Peter Vagy and Martyna Wanat.

The Public Governance Directorate wishes to thank the Chair of the OECD's Public Governance Committee, Dustin Brown (Office of Management and Budget, Government of the United States of America), for his guidance over the course of the preparation of the Policy Framework. The Directorate also wishes to acknowledge the contributions of key international organisations, Member and Partner governments and interested members of the public to successive drafts of the Policy Framework. In particular, the Directorate thanks Australia, Belgium, Brazil, Canada, Chile, the Czech Republic, Denmark, Estonia, France, Germany, Ireland, Italy, Japan, Latvia, Luxembourg, Norway, Poland, Portugal, Slovakia, and Sweden for their comments and for providing examples of country-based practice. The Directorate also thanks the United Nations Committee of Experts on Public Administration (CEPA), the European Commission's Structural Reform Support Service (SRSS), the European Commission's Directorate-General for Neighbourhood and Enlargement Negotiations (DG NEAR), the European Commission's Directorate-General for Human Resources and Security (DG HR), the European Commission's Directorate-General for Budget (DG BUDG), the National Academy of Public Administration (NAPA, USA), the Latin American Development Bank (CAF), the Asian Development Bank (ADB), and such non-governmental organisations as Transparency International (TI), the European Policy Centre (EPC) and the *Centro Latinoamericano de Administración para el Desarrollo* (CLAD), for their contributions.

# Table of contents

Figures

## Boxes

## Follow OECD Publications on:

*http://twitter.com/OECD_Pubs*

*http://www.facebook.com/OECDPublications*

*http://www.linkedin.com/groups/OECD-Publications-4645871*

*http://www.youtube.com/oecdilibrary*

*http://www.oecd.org/oecddirect/*

# Executive Summary

The Policy Framework on Sound Public Governance is divided into two parts:

- Part I: The Values and Enablers of Sound Public Governance
- Part II: Sound Public Governance for Policy Formulation, Implementation and Evaluation

## Part I: The Values and Enablers of Sound Public Governance

The first part of this Framework presents the importance of key governance values in improving the way governments structure relations internally, with external stakeholders, and with citizens. It then provides an overview of enablers of sound public governance that governments can adopt to pursue effective, equitable decision-making and successful reforms.

### The Values of Sound Public Governance

Governance is about meeting the needs of, and improving outcomes for, people. To this end, the OECD suggests building a values-based culture of public governance. While noting that governance values are shaped by a country's specific cultural traditions, the Framework highlights baseline practices in OECD countries that can generate a new culture of governance and orient public decision-making towards the common interest. The OECD pays special attention to:

- *Public sector integrity* as a critical component to prevent corruption, safeguard democratic institutions and guarantee the rule of law.
- *Openness and transparency* policies, as key ingredients to build accountability and trust, which include the accessibility of public information, the proactive disclosure of information and data, and a strategic approach to public communications.
- *Inclusiveness, participation, gender equality and diversity,* which contribute to the quality of democracy and help empower marginalised, disadvantaged and/or vulnerable groups.
- *Accountability and the respect for the rule of law*, which help ensure the efficiency and effectiveness of governments and public institutions, and strengthen citizens' trust. This includes effective and efficient justice systems.

### The Enablers of Sound Public Governance

OECD work on public governance has demonstrated that leaders struggle to build "the business case" for engaging stakeholders in comprehensive reforms, which are often perceived as a means of reducing expenditures rather than of addressing policy challenges.

Despite sector-specific differences, the OECD Recommendations of the Council in the area of public governance reflect a common set of baseline enablers that can contribute to a better definition and implementation of reforms across government, including:

- *Commitment, vision and leadership,* both politically and in the civil service, to ensure the sustainability of reforms across the public sector.
- *Equitable and evidence-informed policy-making,* to prevent unbalanced interest-based influence while strengthening good governance in using evidence in decision-making.
- *Whole-of-government co-ordination,* notably but not exclusively led by the *centre of government,* to ensure a coherent, integrated approach to multidimensional challenges.
- *Innovation and change management* to introduce and implement new ideas by reinforcing the state's strategic agility and its forward-looking nature while enabling it to support society in transitioning to a better future.

## Part II: Sound Public Governance for Policy Formulation, Implementation and Evaluation

Public governance also refers to the formulation, implementation, communication, and evaluation of government policies. The second part of the Framework presents how governments can shape policy-making at different stages of the policy cycle through the strategic use of policy instruments and management tools.

### Toward sound policy formulation and design

While policy-making does not necessarily follow a linear path, the Framework provides guidance on management tools and policy instruments that can support policymakers once a policy challenge has been identified, defined, and framed to determine courses of action.

Evidence suggests that the following **management tools** can improve the quality of policy formulation and design. The Framework stresses the importance of:

- *Strategic planning* to translate political commitments and ambitions into strategies and action plans,
- *Skills for developing policy,* that combine traditional aptitudes with new skills in digital, open and innovative government,
- *Digital capacities* to enable collaboration and enhance transparency,
- *Use of data* to identify or anticipate societal needs and inform policy design.

Governments usually have three main **instruments** at their disposal to achieve their objectives: spending, taxation and regulation. Digital tools and public procurement also provide very powerful avenues for giving effect to policy measures. This chapter highlights the importance of:

- *Regulatory policy and governance* to ensure that regulations meet the desired objectives and new challenges as efficiently as possible.
- *Budgetary governance* to translate political commitments into decisions on what policies receive financing and how these resources are generated.

### Toward sound policy implementation

The Framework assesses key determinants of successful policy **implementation** and underscores the importance of:

- Strengthening the *capacities and skills of public employees,*
- Strengthening *digital government strategies* to enable a more strategic use of government data,
- A well-designed *public procurement system,* which allows to use procurement as a strategic level of policy objectives,

- *Public-private (PPPs) and public-civil partnerships*, to share policy implementation functions and service delivery,
- *Agile and innovative approaches*, to create feedback loops during the implementation and service delivery process,
- *A strategic approach to the implementation of the SDGs.*

Monitoring policy and governance **performance** is essential to ensure the proper implementation of public policies. Monitoring information can feed decision-making and improve performance, helping policymakers track progress and make adjustments when necessary. Monitoring can also promote accountability to stakeholders on issues such as the use of resources, internal processes, and the outputs of a policy. The Framework highlights that:

- OECD countries are increasingly focusing on *monitoring the alignment of policies* as well as their impact.
- *Monitoring the administration's financial performance and budget execution* can help governments assess the effectiveness of public spending against strategic objectives and adjust the allocation of financial resources.
- Many OECD countries *measure regulatory performance* and ensure regulatory compliance works through inspections.

### *Toward robust policy evaluation*

Evaluating performance and policy results helps policymakers understand why some policies work and others do not. If the evidence produced is fed into the policy cycle, policy evaluations can optimise the value for money, accountability and transparency of the policy-making process, and provide legitimacy for the use of public funds and resources. The chapter shows the importance of building institutional frameworks for policy evaluation and promoting the quality and use of evaluation across government. It also highlights the relevance of conducting *ex-post regulatory reviews,* to ensure regulations in place are both relevant and adapted to their aims.

# Introduction: Toward Integrated Sound Public Governance

The Policy Framework on Sound Public Governance (hereafter the Framework) aims to provide governments at all levels with an integrated diagnostic, guidance and benchmarking tool to help:

- Design and implement *public governance reforms* that can lead to improvements in, and the sustainability of, prosperity for their country and the wellbeing of their citizens;
- Design and implement reforms in any policy area by taking *public governance approaches for effective policy-making* into account so that reforms can more effectively respond to complex, multidimensional challenges. This takes on added importance as countries move to adapt the United Nations (UN) Agenda 2030 and implement its Sustainable Development Goals (SDGs) in a way that reflects national conditions;
- Design and pursue a public-governance reform agenda that enables governments to move closer to OECD standards and practices in this area.

The primary target audiences of this Framework include centres of government, line ministries, government agencies and other public institutions in the executive branch at all levels of government, especially when they go about designing, implementing and evaluating policy and governance reform agendas. This Framework could also be useful for civil society to assess governments' participation, decision-making and policy-making arrangements as well as for legislative and judicial branches seeking to modernise their approaches to governance as a means to strengthen capacity to serve citizens and businesses better.

## Why a Framework?

More than ten years after the 2008 financial crisis, and as governments strive to manage the COVID-19 pandemic and its aftermath in a way that optimises and sustains positive outcomes for all citizens, governments are facing increasingly multidimensional policy challenges that require cross-cutting, multifaceted responses in a context of diminishing public resources and low trust levels in government (OECD, 2017[1]).

While the world faces systemic and interconnected challenges such as climate change and growing inequality; governments remain ill-equipped to deal effectively with these issues (OECD, 2017[2]). This new scenario has raised multiple challenges for public administrations. Historical governance problems, such as corruption, excessive red tape, inefficient spending and lack of skills, are now exacerbated by bottlenecks that render more difficult or prevent effective co-ordination across different administrative units and policy areas, and the need to identify, attract and retain new sets of skills and capacities in the public sector to address new political and technological developments effectively. Inadequate design, and poor management of institutions and governance instruments and tools lie at the core of governance failures, preventing governments from achieving their goals for their jurisdiction and its citizens (Meuleman, 2018[3]). For instance, the OECD report on the Governance of Inclusive Growth (2016[4]) found that governance failures may lead to widespread informality in the labour market, limited access to education and a lack of formal safety nets - all of which drive inequality. Failure often involves substantial financial costs to fix problems with subsequent reforms or mitigate the harm caused. Consequently, governance failure can undermine citizens' trust in government.

The environmental, social, and economic challenges of our times call for a multidimensional and integrated approach to public policy and service delivery. It is clear that traditional analytical tools and problem-solving methods are no longer enabling the achievement of better results and outcomes that are demanded by and expected from citizens. Innovative approaches to public governance along with more holistic and integrated strategies are required to enable governments to respond effectively to the multidimensional challenges facing society. This need for a holistic commitment to multidimensional and coherent policy design and implementation, and to the governance arrangements that can deliver on this commitment, is reflected in the United Nations 2030 Agenda for Sustainable Development.

Governments now strive to bolster capacity to tackle complexity and address systemic challenges while responding to immediate-term priorities generated by political imperatives. At the same time, citizens and civil society are demanding a more equitable, open and inclusive culture of governance, one in which decisions are taken in the public interest rather than under the undue influence of powerful interest groups.

While the Policy Framework is not designed to identify governance failures and the root causes behind them, it highlights different baseline practices that reflect good governance because they illustrate governments that work well, without necessarily being at the frontier of governance. These baseline practices have been, and are being, developed and adopted by OECD Members and Partners in a manner that reflects a values-based approach to governance, where resources are obtained and spent efficiently and in the public interest.

## The origins of the Framework

Over more than a decade, notably since the 2008 economic crisis, the OECD, through its Public Governance and Regulatory Policy Committees, has stood witness to, and recorded, the key governance challenges facing national and subnational governments. In so doing, the OECD has accumulated a significant body of evidence from Member and Partner countries and from this evidence has drawn key lessons regarding what works and what does not in terms of the policy responses that have best addressed these governance challenges. In many areas of public governance, the OECD has enshrined principles and good practices emerging from this body of evidence in a number of OECD legal instruments in public governance.[1] These instruments embody principles and good practices across key thematic areas of public governance – practices that country-based evidence suggests work best in enabling governments to effectively address the challenges they face in each area (Figure 0.1).

Figure 0.1. OECD legal instruments under the responsibility of the OECD's Regulatory Policy Committee and Public Governance Committee

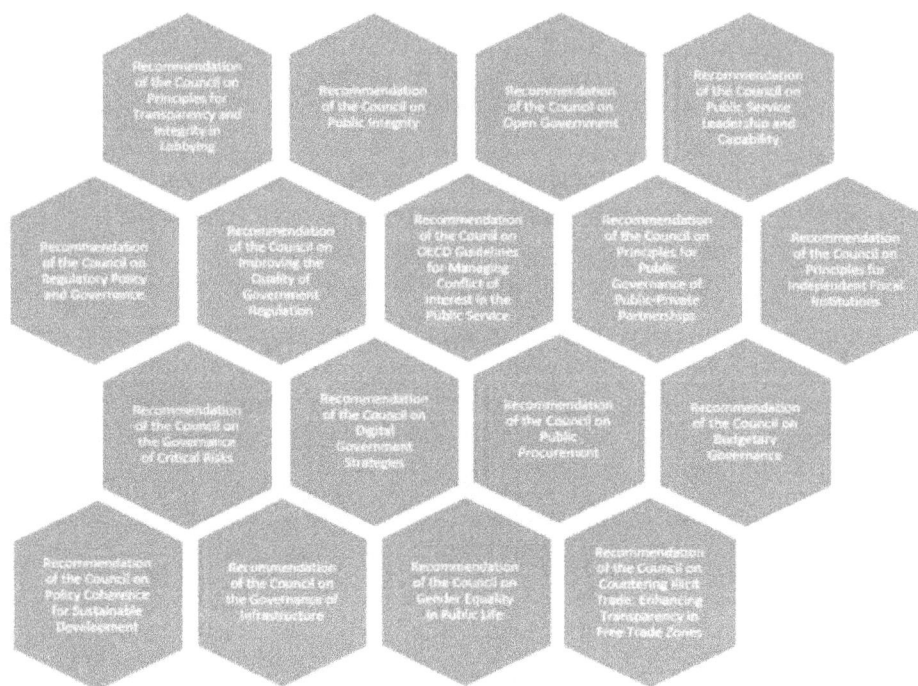

Source: OECD Legal Instruments, https://legalinstruments.oecd.org/en/

The main observations and key lessons learned from over two decades' worth of effort by governments in designing and implementing public governance reforms include:

- The existence of a significant gap in evidence on how public governance can improve inclusive-growth outcomes;
- Reform leaders struggle with building a business case to engage in comprehensive public governance reform; as it is often seen as a tool to reduce expenditures rather than a means to solve complex policy challenges;
- Top-down approaches devoid of engagement with citizens and civil society usually limit the success of the reform;
- A coherent, integrated, systems-based approach to reform can lead to better results as it allows for the identification of synergies, trade-offs and sequencing considerations.

The genesis of this Framework stems from an initial discussion of these observations during a meeting of the Public Governance Committee (PGC) in 2013. PGC delegates recognised that significant efforts were being made to codify policy recommendations by area (e.g.: regulatory policy and governance, transparency and integrity in lobbying). At the same time, the discussion underscored that what was missing was a narrative that tied it all together coherently in way that could help governments adopt integrated approaches to public governance. Delegates concluded that an integrated narrative could help governments identify trade-offs and sequencing considerations in a governance-reform agenda, thereby enabling governments to prioritise governance-reform initiatives coherently and allocate resources to implement them in a way that sustains impact and optimises positive outcomes.

This Framework builds on these lessons learned and on practices gathered over the past decade through the OECD's Public Governance Reviews (PGRs) and other country- and sector-specific assessments in public governance. It weaves together a narrative that links together baseline features of sound public governance in the existing OECD legal instruments in public governance while highlighting evidence of emerging good practice in areas of public governance in which no OECD instruments yet exist (for example whole-of-government coordination or evaluating policy performance). The Framework builds on similar exercises developed by the OECD, such as the OECD / EU SIGMA Principles of Public Administration (SIGMA, 2017[5]), and other international organisations such as the UN Economic and Social Council's Principles of effective governance for sustainable development (2018[6]) and the European Commission Quality of Public Administration Toolkit (2017[71]). Most importantly, the Framework reflects a broad consultation process with international organisations and civil society organisations, with OECD Members, and with the general public.

## What is Sound Public Governance for the OECD?

Sound public governance consists of the formal and informal rules, procedures, practices and interactions within the State, and between the State, non-state institutions and citizens, that frame the exercise of public authority and decision-making in the public interest.

Sound public governance constitutes a *sine qua non* condition for pluralist democracies to give effect to the respect for the rule of law and human rights. Efficient democratic institutions lie at the core of sound public governance.

Sound public governance is therefore the combination of three interconnected elements:

- **Values:** context-based principles of behaviour that guide public governance across all of its dimensions in a way that advances and upholds the public interest.
- **Enablers:** an integrated nexus of practices that support the effective definition and implementation of reforms.
- **Instruments and tools:** a set of public policies and management practices for efficient governance and policy implementation.

Figure 0.2. Elements of Sound Public Governance

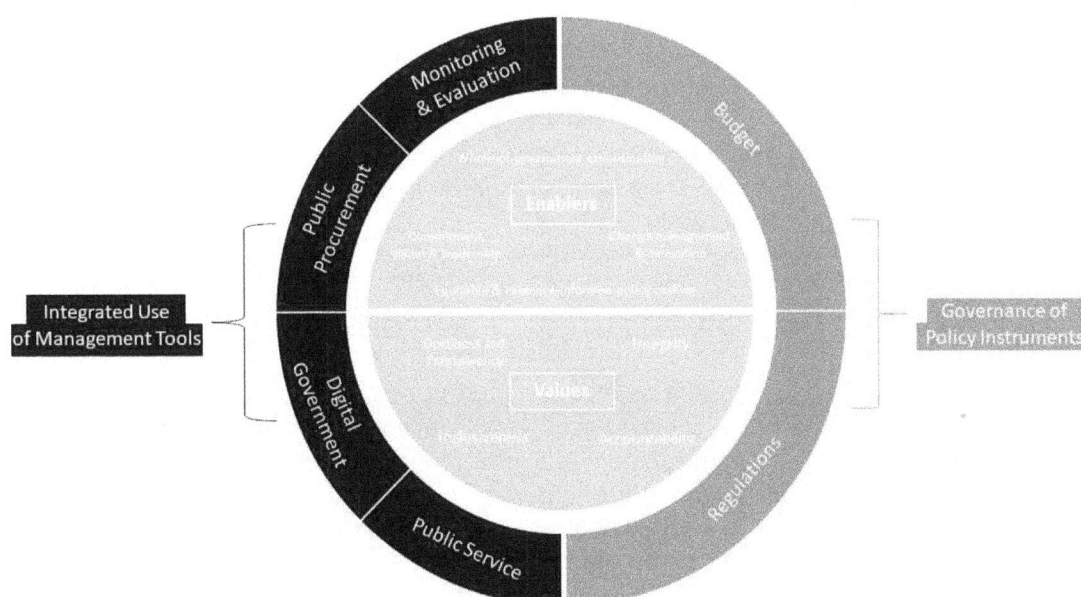

*Source*: Authors' own elaboration

The values, enablers, instruments and tools that underpin sound public governance are to a large extent, mutually interdependent. A sound budgetary policy calls for transparency, participative and integrity measures, as well as for the development of sound monitoring and evaluation tools. Digital government strategies require effective organisational, governance and regulatory frameworks. A whole-of-government regulatory framework necessitates sound co-ordination, stakeholder engagement mechanisms, and management capacity.

## How does the Framework work?

While the Framework's main target audience is the executive branch of government, the content of the Framework can resonate beyond the executive and encourage collaboration across branches and jurisdictions from a whole-of-society perspective.

At the conclusion of each chapter, the Framework poses a small number of questions that readers can use to assess their government's institutional and decision-making capacity in key public governance areas. The Framework also provides, where possible, reform-implementation guidance based on the toolkits developed to support the implementation of existing Recommendations as well as evidence on trends and practices drawn from the OECD's broader work with Member and Partner countries.

In practical terms, the Framework is expected to be used:

- As an assessment and benchmarking tool to spotlight specific governance areas for reform and to identify, when pursuing a specific reform, which other governance practices are important to take into consideration (for instance, an open government framework can contribute to the effectiveness of a regulatory policy and vice-versa).
- As a discussion tool to engage with different actors within the State and from civil society in governance assessments and reforms.
- As a guidance tool to pursue reforms, through the provision of resources and links to more specific and detailed information about OECD international standards, toolkits and comparative data on governance areas.

The Framework is intended to complement existing OECD legal instruments in the area of public governance; these instruments will remain the applicable legal standards on public governance at the OECD with their implementation monitored regularly by the relevant committee and reported on to the OECD Council. The Framework will support the implementation of these legal instruments by setting out an integrated vision of public governance that weaves together a coherent and integrated narrative that runs through the OECD's *acquis* in this area.

## What is the Framework not about?

This Framework is not seeking to impose a univocal vision of, or single recipe for, public governance; nor does it seek to gloss over the many context-based factors affecting the capacity of governments to integrate these practices into public management (e.g. size of country and government; homogeneity of the civil service; level of government; etc.). Additionally, while it intends to provide a holistic approach to public governance, it is not exhaustive. As it primarily presents OECD work in the area, it does not include important elements on which the OECD has gathered limited evidence, for instance on the internal organisation of specific ministries or administrative units, the governance of addressing major public security challenges or managing the emergence of societies from conflict, which are particularly context-based. That said the Framework's key values, enablers, instruments and tools can potentially be adapted to assist governments in addressing these challenges as well.

## The future of the Framework

The Framework as a tool is designed to be evergreen and easily updatable as practices evolve, new evidence is collected, and current OECD legal instruments are revised or new ones adopted. Forthcoming editions therefore aim to present new examples of good governance that illustrate the frontier of practice reflecting sound public governance. Indeed, future editions of the Framework may include time-bound performance indicators to assess the maturity of governance systems. The objective of embedding possible "maturity models" related to governance practice, notably linked to the assessment questions presented at the end of the chapter sections, would be to provide practical, indicator-based tools for governments to monitor and evaluate their progress in moving closer to the frontier of OECD standards in the areas of public governance highlighted in the Framework. The OECD hopes that these future editions will continue to be useful to Member and Partner countries alike, as governments advance toward the frontier of sound practice in the various areas of public governance.

With this Framework, the OECD seeks to bear witness to the different practices that countries have developed – and continue to develop – to ensure that their institutional and decision-making arrangements lead to improving results for people: *better policies – through better governance – for better lives.*

## References

European Commission (2017), Toolbox 2017 edition - Quality of Public administration, Publications Office of the European Union,Luxembourg, http://dx.doi.org/10.2767/483489    [71]

Meuleman, L. (2018), *Metagovernance for sustainability : a framework for implementing the Sustainable Development Goals*, Routledge.    [3]

OECD (2017), *Government at a Glance 2017*, OECD Publishing, Paris, https://dx.doi.org/10.1787/gov_glance-2017-en.    [1]

OECD (2017), *Systems Approaches to Public Sector Challenges: Working with Change*, OECD Publishing, Paris, https://dx.doi.org/10.1787/9789264279865-en.    [2]

OECD (2016), *The Governance of Inclusive Growth*, OECD Publishing, Paris, https://dx.doi.org/10.1787/9789264257993-en.    [4]

SIGMA (2017), *The Principles of Public Administration 2017 edition*, http://www.oecd.org/termsandconditions. (accessed on 4 October 2019).    [5]

United Nations (2018), *Principles of effective governance for sustainable development*, Economic and Social Council, Official Recors 2018, Supplement No. 24, E/2018/44-E/C.16/2018/8, para. 3.    [6]

Note

---

[1] The Public Governance Committee and Regulatory Policy Committee are responsible for a combined seventeen OECD Council Recommendations and one Declaration. For the full list, please visit: https://legalinstruments.oecd.org/en/instruments?mode=advanced&committeeIds=863,7497&dateType=adoption.

# Part I The Values and Enablers of Sound Public Governance

# 1 The Values of Sound Public Governance

Building a values-based culture of sound public governance is a continuous and challenging process of shaping organisational and individual practices and behaviour. While governance values are always context-dependent, this chapter highlights key values that aim to generate a new culture of governance, which can positively influence the manner in which governments select and prioritise policy problems, contribute to prevent corruption and policy capture, and orient public decision-making towards the common interest. The values discussed in this chapter are integrity; openness and transparency; inclusiveness, participation, gender equality and diversity; and finally accountability and respect for the rule of law. This chapter argues that while there is no perfect reform recipe, concrete steps can be taken to move the public sector, both culturally and institutionally, toward more values-based performance.

Governments around the world are increasingly coming under scrutiny and pressure. In a context in which the effects of the 2007-2008 financial crisis on such vital policy challenges as inequality, poverty, and corruption have yet to recede, the public sector as a whole in both Member and Partner countries is being challenged to deliver more with less and demonstrate to citizens that their lives are improving thanks to how the government is spending public resources.

Citizens are more and more concerned about corruption as one of the most corrosive issues of our time. It wastes public resources, widens economic and social inequalities, breeds discontent and political polarisation and reduces trust in institutions[1]. In recognising the benefits of the digital transformation, citizens are calling for governments that are more transparent and responsive, and that adopt more and new forms of stakeholder participation in the policy-making and resource-allocation process.

Sound Public Governance constitutes a *sine qua non* condition for countries to meet these new challenges and to give effect to the increasing demands from citizens. A set of key public governance values, along with effective democratic institutions, lie at the core of sound public governance: they constitute indispensable means to engage in open, equitable and inclusive decision-making in the public interest and in partnership with citizens to enhance wellbeing and prosperity for all. Sound public governance is therefore not an end in itself but a process to improve individual and societal outcomes.

---

### Box 1.1. Definition of Sound Public Governance

Sound public governance consists of the formal and informal rules, procedures, practices and interactions within the State, and between the State, non-state institutions and citizens, that frame the exercise of public authority and decision-making in the public interest.

Sound public governance constitutes a sine qua non condition for pluralist democracies to give effect to the respect for the rule of law and human rights, with efficient democratic institutions lying at the core of sound public governance.

Sound public governance is therefore the combination of three interconnected elements:

- *Values:* context-dependent principles of behaviour that guide public governance across all of its dimensions in a way that advances and sustain the public interest.
- *Enablers:* an integrated nexus of practices that supports the effective design and implementation of reforms.

*Instruments and tools:* a set of policies and management practices for efficient governance and policy and service design, implementation and evaluation.

---

The shared goal of sustainable development, expressed in **the UN Agenda 2030 Sustainable Development Goals (SDGs)**, defines a clear set of commitments within goal 16 to achieve peace, justice and strong institutions. SDG 16 includes the creation of peaceful and inclusive societies that guarantee access to justice for all along with effective, accountable and transparent public institutions at all levels of government. These commitments include such targets as the reduction of corruption and bribery in all their forms; guaranteeing rights of minorities; ensuring responsive, inclusive, participatory and representative decision-making at all levels; guaranteeing freedom of the press and public access to information; and protecting fundamental rights and freedoms of the individual in accordance with national legislation and international agreements.

A proactive stance to these basic commitments is more important now than ever. Countries around the world are increasingly facing challenges to traditional democratic pluralism on both the right and the left of the political spectrum; only an OECD average of 43% of people still trust their governments (OECD, 2017[7]). This is partly the outcome of a deepening disconnect between people and their political systems, while the role of traditional representative democratic channels, such as trade unions or political parties, is being questioned *inter alia* through lower participation rates in the democratic process. The impact on restoring trust in public institutions and on delivering better outcomes of other more direct channels of participation, such as the effect of public consultations using social media on the quality of democracy, is for its part not yet clear.

While the causal links between different factors and trust are not always as clear as often presented, the OECD Trustlab's research finds that high level government integrity is the governmental characteristic most strongly associated with trust in government (Murtin et al., 2018[8]). Moreover, evidence suggests that an administration's efficiency and effectiveness (addressed in greater detail in Part II) in delivering policies and services that actually meet the needs of citizens are governmental characteristics that are strongly associated with trust in government. However, confidence in public institutions is also determined by other factors.

Trust is also about citizens being able to rely with confidence on a "social bargain" that assumes that political and policy decisions are being made in the public interest and that problems requiring government intervention are being addressed in the public interest. Accordingly, the OECD Trustlab's research (Murtin et al., 2018[8]) finds that important determinants of trust in government include satisfaction with government services and with the responsiveness and reliability of government. A lack of trust erodes democracy and compromises the willingness of citizens and businesses to commit to public policies. Lack of trust therefore represents a barrier to inclusive social and economic development to secure prosperity and well-being for all (OECD, 2017[7]).

Government efforts to strengthen – and sometimes rebuild – essential democratic bonds require harnessing a governance culture based on public values that reflect a society's goals and aspirations. Those values are context-dependent and are rooted in historical and cultural traditions that represent the broadest of societal consensus; this consensus can take decades, sometimes centuries, to crystallise. In their pursuit of sound public governance over the past decades, OECD countries have identified and committed themselves to set of governance values. These values are of course interconnected through their common focus on promoting and defending the public interest in pursuit of inclusive growth and development outcomes.

While boundaries between them are difficult to draw, some of the public values being promoted by countries can be clustered around the four axes of **integrity; openness; inclusiveness and accountability**. The values mirror, *inter alia*, the open government principles, defined in the *OECD Recommendation on Open Government* (2017) [OECD/LEGAL/0438] as transparency (including openness), integrity, accountability and stakeholder participation (including inclusiveness). These interconnected and mutually reinforcing values, along with the goal of **effectiveness**, are cornerstones that serve to structure and orient the public sector toward serving citizens' needs in a manner that is free of corruption. These values align with the principles of effective governance for sustainable development adopted by the UN Economic and Social Council (ECOSOC) in July 2018 (United Nations, 2018[6]). Moreover, key values such as **flexibility, agility and responsiveness** can also underpin a public governance system, and many of the practices presented in this framework – for instance in the areas of open government, innovation, and digital government – can contribute to upholding these values.

Building a values-based culture of sound public governance is a continuous and challenging process of shaping organisational and individual practice and behaviour through the identification, design, implementation and evaluation of systemic multifaceted public-governance reforms. Even though there is no perfect (or single) reform recipe, concrete steps can be taken to move the public sector, both culturally and institutionally, toward more democratic, values-based behaviour as a means to serve citizens better, generate inclusive growth and rebuild trust. To guide governments in their endeavour of creating a values-driven public sector, where values guide a results-oriented and citizens-centred culture, leadership and policy and service design, the first pillar of the *OECD Recommendation on Public Service Leadership and Capability* (2019[9]) [OECD/LEGAL/0445] offers concrete guidance. For example, by including a statement of values in the public sector code, Canada aims to ensure that certain values act as a compass to guide the professional behaviour of officials (Box 1.2).

---

### Box 1.2. Values-based culture of sound public governance

Canada uses the following statement of values within its public sector code: "These values are a compass to guide public servants in everything they do. They cannot be considered in isolation from each other as they will often overlap. This Code and respective organizational codes of conduct are important sources of guidance for public servants. Organizations are expected to take steps to integrate these values into their decisions, actions, policies, processes and systems. Similarly, public servants can expect to be treated in accordance with these values by their organisation."

Source: Example of country practice provided by the Government of Canada as part of the Policy Framework's consultation process

---

Evidence also suggests that reforms that aim to create or strengthen a values-based culture of sound public governance cannot be implemented through siloed or sector-based approaches. Crosscutting, multidimensional reform strategies forged through **robust co-ordination** across government silos to incorporate all relevant strands seem to work best.

Most of the practices that the evidence suggests work have been embodied in OECD legal instruments on public governance: the *Recommendation on Improving the Quality of Government Regulation* (1995) [OECD/LEGAL/0278], the *Recommendation on Guidelines for Managing Conflict of Interest in the Public Service* (2003) [OECD/LEGAL/0316], the *Recommendation on Regulatory Policy and Governance* (2012) [OECD/LEGAL/0390], the *Recommendation on Budgetary Governance (2015)* [OECD/LEGAL/0410], the *Recommendation on Gender Equality in the Public Life* (2015) [OECD/LEGAL/0418], the *Recommendation on Public Integrity* (2017) [OECD/LEGAL/0435], and the *Recommendation on Open Government* (2017) [OECD/LEGAL/0438].

## Integrity

**Integrity** is the cornerstone of any system of sound public governance. It is vital for governing in the public interest for the prosperity and well-being of society as a whole. It reinforces such fundamental values as the commitment to a pluralistic democracy based on the rule of law and respect for human rights.

That said, no country is immune to violations of integrity, and corruption remains one of the most challenging issues facing governments today. Integrity risks exist in the various interactions between the public sector, civil society and individuals at all stages of the political and policy process. More than the act of bribery, violations of integrity standards are becoming increasingly complex and include a wide range of practices such as conflict of interests, trading in influence, and embezzlement of public property, often associated with more subtle practices such as undue influence on decision-making processes resulting in policy capture. It includes a wide range of practices such as bribery, state capture and embezzlement, often associated with other illegal practices such as money laundering or bid-rigging. Corruption erodes public governance and democracy, and citizens' confidence in them, because it wastes public resources, widens economic and social inequalities, and breeds discontent and political polarisation (OECD, 2017[11]).

Building an integrity system in the public sector is a critical component not only in preventing corruption but also in safeguarding democratic institutions and the rule of law. A strategic and sustainable response to corruption therefore places public integrity at its core (Box 1.3).

---

### Box 1.3. Definition of Public Integrity

"Public Integrity refers to the consistent alignment of, and adherence to, shared ethical values, principles and norms for upholding and prioritising the public interest over private interests in public-sector behaviour and decision-making."

Source: OECD (2017[11]), OECD Recommendation of the Council on Public Integrity [OECD/LEGAL/0435], http://www.oecd.org/gov/ethics/OECD-Recommendation-Public-Integrity.pdf.

---

Over the years, OECD Member countries have adopted legal and institutional frameworks to strengthen integrity in the public sector. For instance in 2009, parties to the Convention on Combating Bribery of Foreign Public Officials in International Business Transactions [OECD/LEGAL/0293] agreed to put in place new measures to bolster their efforts to prevent, detect and investigate foreign bribery through the adoption of the OECD Recommendation for Further Combating Bribery of Foreign Public Officials in International business Transactions (2009[12]) [OECD/LEGAL/0378]. Yet, many countries rely heavily (or solely) on compliance and enforcement mechanisms. Such approaches usually stress the importance of both increasing the costs and lowering the benefits of undesired behaviour through controls and sanctions. The aim is to reduce the discretion of decision makers in order to diminish their scope for misbehaviour. However, evidence suggests that the effects of overly-rigid compliance regimes tend to be limited and fail to act as a deterrent on a person's behaviour (Box 1.4).

Box 1.4. The hidden costs of control

A series of behavioural experiments, looking at the effects of compliance programmes on a person's intrinsic motivation for integrity, found that some of the more traditional methods of control were, in fact, promoting corruption rather than preventing it.

For example, the "four-eye principle" requires approval by at least two equally responsible individuals and is based on the argument that it is harder to successfully corrupt two people than it is to corrupt one. However, experimental evidence has found that involving additional actors to a decision-making process without giving them a unique responsibility might not necessarily be an effective approach to promoting integrity.

Indeed, the principle is motivated by distrust and can have adverse impact on employees' intrinsic motivations. Moreover, it enables the diffusion of responsibility between individuals, taking away moral responsibility from the individual decision. The principle also encourages people to develop solidarity with one another and can entrap them in a corrupt network.

Source: Schikora, J (2011[13]), "Bringing the four-eyes-principle to the lab.", Münchener Wirtschaftswissenschaftliche Beiträge: VWL: discussion papers, http://www.econbiz.de/Record/bringing-the-four-eyes-principle-to-the-lab-schikora-jantheodor/

The *OECD Recommendation on Public Integrity* (2017[11]) [OECD/LEGAL/0435] incorporates much of the existing knowledge on integrity practices in the public sector, but shifts the focus from ad hoc integrity policies to a context-dependent, evidence and risk-based approach with emphasis on promoting a cultural change and examining integrity policy-making through a behavioural lens. The *Recommendation on Public Integrity* includes a number of new crosscutting considerations and promotes coherence with other key elements of public governance. For example, it highlights the need for effective coordination across institutions and levels of government to harness each relevant area of responsibility in the design and delivery of a coherent, integrated public-sector integrity framework. Moreover, as risks to integrity can be caused by interactions between the public sector, the private sector and civil society, the *Recommendation on Public Integrity* incorporates a whole-of-society approach tailored to the specific integrity risks of sectors, organisations and officials.

In particular, the *Recommendation on Public Integrity* (2017[11]) [OECD/LEGAL/0435] provides guidance to policymakers for developing a public integrity strategy that is built on three pillars: (i) building a coherent and comprehensive integrity system, (ii) cultivating a culture of public integrity, and (iii) enabling accountability and transparency (Figure 1.1). This public integrity strategy goes beyond mitigating corruption risks towards a vision for public integrity that strives to develop solutions adapted to the causes of integrity problems.

Figure 1.1. The three pillars of the OECD Recommendation on Public Integrity: System, culture, accountability

A **coherent and comprehensive public integrity system** aims to ensure that policymakers develop a set of interconnected policies and tools that are coordinated and avoid overlaps and gaps:

- The growing empirical evidence gathered by behavioural scientists shows that emphasising commitments at the highest political and management levels sets the tone for how integrity is perceived across the public sector and society (OECD, 2018[14]).

- Similarly, ensuring that institutional responsibilities across the public sector are clearly identified not only increases the effectiveness of the overall integrity system but also strengthens the integrity of individual decision-makers. Integrity is not only the responsibility of ethics officers, but also of those working across a broad range of government functions, including public procurement, human resource management, public financial management, taxation, and education. The actors responsible span both central and subnational levels of government, as well as function within each public sector organisation. Figure 1.2. shows some of the mechanisms that government uses to mainstream integrity policies across line ministries.

- In OECD Member countries, the Centre of Government often leads inter-institutional coordination among public officials, across administrative silos and between levels of government in designing, implementing and evaluating the performance of integrity frameworks.

Figure 1.2. Mechanisms to mainstream integrity policies across line ministries

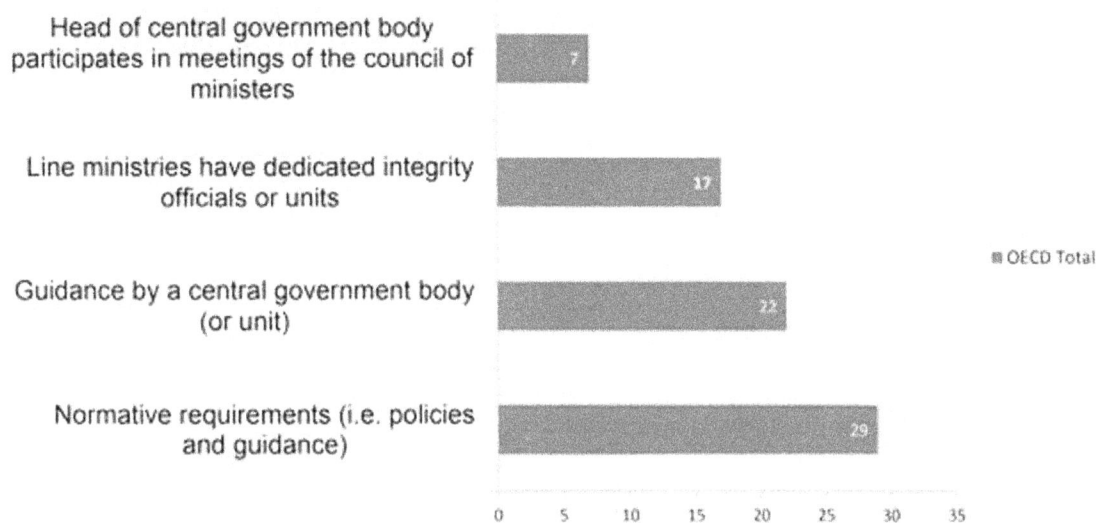

*Source: OECD (2016), Survey on Public Sector Integrity, OECD, Paris.*

A growing number of OECD Member countries have recognised the importance of developing a strategic, risk-based approach and setting high standards of conduct to promote values-based decisions in the public sector and society. For example, codes of conduct (Box 1.5) define behaviour expectations and prioritise adherence to public-service values to reflect integrity in the overarching strategy, as well as in management goals and performance appraisals. Additionally, clear and proportionate procedures to help prevent violations of public integrity standards and manage potential conflicts of interest may be put in place.

---

**Box 1.5. Codes of conduct for civil servants in Denmark**

In 2007, the Danish government issued the Code of Conduct in the Public Sector to clarify the basic duties and responsibilities of public sector employees. In 2015, the Danish ministry of Finance launched Code VII-Seven Key Duties targeted more specifically at employees and managers in central government to supplement the Code of Conduct. Code VII describes seven key duties of civil servants in central government as follows:

- Legality
- Truthfulness
- Professionalism
- Development and cooperation
- Responsibility and management
- Openness about errors
- Party-political neutrality

A revised edition of the Code of conduct in the Public Sector was published in 2017. It reflects Code VII guidelines, as well as the Local Government Denmark's Code of Quality and Ethics in the Public Administration which contains recommendations for the relationship between local politicians and the

---

public administration. Additionally, reference is made to the Ministry of justice's guide How to Avoid Corruption.

Source: Agency for modernization, Local Government Denmark and Danish Regions (2017[15]) Code of Conduct in the Public Sector https://modst.dk/media/18742/code-of-conduct-in-the-public-sectorforside.pdf ; Denmark Ministry of Finance, (2015[16]) seven key duties for civil servants in central government, www.modst.dk/kodexvii

**Cultivating a culture of integrity**, aims to appeal to the intrinsic motivation of individuals to behave ethically – in the public sector, the private sector, and in society as a whole:

- Where appropriate, awareness campaigns and educational programmes for children and youth (OECD, 2018[17])can enable a whole-of-society culture of integrity that engages the private sector, civil-society organisations and citizens to exercise more readily their roles and responsibilities in preventing and fighting corrupt practices. More targeted approaches engaging the private sector and civil society on the benefits that arise from upholding integrity, e.g. through regulations on conflict of interest and job transitions in business and non-profit activities can also be very fruitful.

- Leadership behaviours and good stewardship are crucial to promote a culture of integrity. Therefore, governments and public entities in OECD Member countries also increasingly invest in the integrity leadership of public managers, reinforce the merit-based public service, for example by integrating integrity into job-selection processes, and provide guidance and training programmes for public officials.

- The pillar also includes supporting an open organisational culture where ethical dilemmas, public integrity concerns and errors are discussed freely and resolved in a timely manner. Awareness-raising activities on reporting violations of integrity are therefore crucial to change the culture around whistleblowing and break down negative connotations associated with it.

**Enabling effective accountability** builds on risk-based controls and real responsibility for integrity violations:

- It involves applying an effective internal control and risk-management framework to reduce the vulnerability of public organisations to fraud and corruption, whilst contributing to a culture of integrity. In addition, developing effective enforcement responses to all suspected integrity violations ensures the coherence and legitimacy of an integrity system and is the principal means by which societies can ensure compliance and deter misconduct. It demonstrates the government's commitment to uphold integrity values and helps to instil these values in individuals, organisations and society as cultural norms.

- External oversight and control mechanisms foster the public integrity system's effectiveness, notably through adequate responses of public officials to oversight bodies' recommendations, effective complains and allegation handling procedures, and impartial enforcement of laws and regulations throughout the public sector.. For example, Supreme Audit Institutions (SAIs) are important actors of a country's accountability chain. They can promote effective accountability through a wide range of tools, including audits and recommendations. Traditionally known for their oversight of public expenditure, their roles are evolving to inform governments on what works and what does not in public governance (OECD, 2016[18]). Moreover, SAIs can develop work specifically designed to promote public integrity, such as incorporating ethics issues checks when conducting audits.

- Internal Audit institutions increase citizen's ability to hold public sector entities accountable through objective assessments of public resource management.

- Transparency and participation in the public integrity system are important drivers of accountability. An accountability ecosystem approach recognises the role played by different state and non-state actors – and the complementarities that exist among them – in fostering public scrutiny. Ensuring inclusive and fair participation of different interests in decision-making processes is a key tool to avoid policy capture of public policies by narrow interest groups. To that end, Governments can develop conflict-of-interest management frameworks as well as guarantee effective regulations and practices for integrity and transparency in lobbying activities and in the financing of political parties and elections campaigns. The *Recommendation on Principles for Transparency and Integrity in Lobbying* (OECD, 2010[19]) [OECD/LEGAL/0379] and the *Recommendation on OECD Guidelines for Managing Conflict of Interest in the Public Service* (OECD, 2003[20]) [OECD/LEGAL/0316] provide clear roadmaps to address these issues.

---

### Box 1.6. United Kingdom Register of People with Significant Control

On 6 April 2016, the United Kingdom became the first G20 country to require private companies to create a People with Significant Control (PSC) register and make that information publicly available. People with significant control, or beneficial owners, are the person or persons who ultimately own or control the company and benefit from it. The information is available in open-data format on the Companies House website. Registers of beneficial ownership aim to tackle crimes such as tax evasion, corruption and money laundering by preventing people from hiding assets and income.

Source: Mor, F. (2019[21]), "Registers of beneficial ownership", House of Commons Library Briefing Paper No. 8259, London: House of Commons library. https://researchbriefings.files.parliament.uk/documents/CBP-8259/CBP-8259.pdf.

---

## Core questions for consideration

- *System*: Does the legislative and institutional framework enable public sector organisations, public officials and leaders to take responsibilities for integrity? Do leaders and managers at the highest levels demonstrate commitment to integrity and a high standard of propriety in carrying out their official duties? Is coordination between different actors across the integrity system at the central and subnational levels ensured? Is there a clear, memorable and actionable statement of public sector values that is communicated internally and externally?

- Culture: Are there measures to promote a culture of integrity in government (e.g. merit-based recruitment, training opportunities on integrity issues, awareness raising, reporting channels)? Does the public integrity system recognise the role of companies and civil society organisations in upholding and promoting a culture of integrity? Are there measures to promote a culture of integrity in society (e.g. awareness raising and education programmes, codes of conduct/responsible business conduct practices, etc.)?

- Accountability: Is there a strategic approach to risk management and assessing integrity risks? Are policies and practices for identifying, assessing and mitigating integrity risks supported by tools and methodologies and aligned with control activities? How is the coherence, objectivity and timeliness of enforcement mechanisms ensured? Are there regulations or measures in place to manage effectively conflicts of interests? Are there measures to ensure transparency and integrity and lobbying activities, and to instil transparency in the financing of political parties and electoral campaigns?

## Openness and transparency

Openness and transparency policies include the accessibility of information as well as other public resources and the proactive disclosure of information and data. They are key ingredients to build accountability and trust and crucial for the proper functioning of democracies and market economies. Given the importance of openness and transparency in governance and policy-making, open government strategies and initiatives have become a key pillar of public-governance reforms. The OECD defines **open government** (OG) as a culture of public governance that promotes the principles of transparency, integrity, accountability and stakeholder participation in support of democracy and inclusive growth (OECD, 2017[22]). These reforms can range from initiatives to ensure access to public information, to more complex practices to increase **accountability** and **stakeholder participation** in decision-making.

Open government is not an end in itself; it is a tool to achieve policy objectives. Open government principles and practices can be applied to policy-making and service-delivery, regardless of the theme or sector, and across all Branches of Power (when open government frameworks and principles are adopted by a country's Legislative and Judicial Branches or by independent public institutions in addition to the Executive, the OECD refers to the concept of an open state). When policies are decided, designed and implemented in a transparent and inclusive way, they contribute to building citizens' trust and to achieving policy outcomes more effectively, because openness allows governments to broaden the range of input for decision-making. In this regard, the proactive disclosure of clear, complete, timely, reliable and relevant public sector data and information that is free of cost, available in an open and non-proprietary machine-readable format, easy to find, understand, use and reuse, and disseminated through a multi-channel approach is paramount. In this context, also guaranteeing a citizen's right to request government information becomes vital.

Open government can contribute to political equality and inclusiveness too, because it requires governments to reach out to those populations and sectors that are less prone to public participation. For this reason, OECD Recommendations in different areas of public governance, from regulatory policy to public integrity and digital government, advocate for the adoption of open government principles and practices.

By highlighting evidence on those practices that work best in this area across OECD Member countries, the *OECD Recommendation on Open Government* (2017[22]) [OECD/LEGAL/0438] advises that governments develop, adopt and implement open government strategies and initiatives that promote the principles of transparency, integrity, accountability and stakeholder participation in designing and delivering public policies and services. In this regard, policy makers could:

- **Ensure the existence of an enabling environment**, such as the design and implementation of a robust open government legal and regulatory framework, ensuring human, financial, and technical resources and promoting open government literacy;
  - o The success of open government strategies depends largely on the existence of a policy and legal framework that sets the rules for both government and stakeholders, such as the existence of access-to-information frameworks and the protection of civic space. Successful implementation of open government strategies are often coupled with the strategic use of digital government and public sector innovation tools.
- **Develop an implementation framework**, through co-ordination mechanisms across government; monitoring, evaluation and learning mechanisms for open government strategies and initiatives; as well as stakeholder participation processes. In addition, effective communication can support the OG implementation framework as communication serves not just as a means of informing the public, but as a strategic tool to support policy-making and service delivery by enhancing transparency and participation.

- o Since an open government strategy cuts across different policy sectors and public governance areas, the active role of the Centre of Government can be instrumental in providing leadership and effective policy co-ordination. According to the 2016 OECD Survey on Open Government and Citizen Participation, 85% of the surveyed countries have a dedicated office responsible for horizontal co-ordination of open government initiatives (OECD, 2016[23]). Moreover, a sound monitoring and evaluation system for open government initiatives can be pivotal to ensure that policies are achieving their intended outcomes, make corrections if needed and therefore enable open-government initiatives to generate greater impact. However, this is a challenging task: while 91% of countries say they monitor open government initiatives, only half evaluate them (OECD, 2016[23]).

- **Plan a way forward** by exploring the potential of moving from the concept of open government toward that of open state. While adopting a 'whole of state' approach is ideal, it is dependent on the respective political system.

  - o An increasing number of countries are moving from the concept of open government toward that of an open state, as mentioned above. **An open state** tends to be pursued on a collaborative basis, with the Executive, Legislature, Judiciary, independent public institutions, and all levels of government collaborating to exploit synergies and share good practices and lessons learned among themselves and with other stakeholders to promote open government principles.

  - o **Subnational levels of government** have a fundamental role to play in enhancing the policies, values and culture of open government and can make an important contribution to a country's move towards an open state. Historically, they have been at the forefront of open government and innovation practices. Planning the way ahead, further efforts are needed to integrate them in the design and implementation of national strategies and policies.

  - o **Supporting media ecosystems** that are diverse and transparent ultimately promote the open government principles of transparency and accountability. Governments should therefore pursue policies that foster media literacy; independent, local, regional and community-owned media providers; public service media; etc. Such activities are also important in helping governments respond to the changing nature of how the public receives and shares information, as well as resilience to the threats posed by disinformation.

---

Box 1.7. The importance of pursuing transparency

Transparency is critical to include citizens in policy-making and to build trust in public institutions. The opening-up of government processes, proceedings, documents and data for public scrutiny and involvement is a prerequisite to achieve better stakeholder engagement, inclusiveness, integrity and accountability in public governance. In this regard, the OECD, through its Recommendation on Open Government (2017), suggests that governments should make available clear, complete, timely, reliable and relevant public sector data and information that is free of cost, available in an open and non-proprietary machine-readable format. The OECD also recommends governments to adopt transparent practices in other public governance areas such as public integrity, budgeting, public procurement and regulatory policy.

Source: OECD Recommendation of the Council on Open Government (2017[22]) [OECD/LEGAL/0438].

Core questions for consideration

- To optimise the benefits that an open government culture can generate, is the appropriate enabling environment in place, including institutional, legal and regulatory frameworks, human, financial and technical resources, and oversight mechanisms to ensure their implementation?

- Are policies planned and implemented in collaboration with citizens and all relevant stakeholders and are they associated with monitoring, evaluation and learning mechanisms to ensure impact? Are these frameworks being applied to regional and local governments? To the other Branches of the State?

- To what extent does the government proactively make available clear, complete, timely, reliable and relevant public sector data and information that is free of cost, available in an open and non-proprietary machine-readable format, easy to find, understand, use and reuse?

- Does the government fully capture the value of digital technologies for more open and innovative government?

- When developing inclusive stakeholder participation initiatives, is timely, accessible communication considered as integral to this process, and are innovative approaches used to ensure inclusiveness and representativeness?

## Inclusiveness, Participation, Gender Equality and Diversity

In keeping with the core theme of Agenda 2030 "Leaving no one behind", governments can take active measures to design, apply, and monitor **equality in governance and decision-making**, with a special focus on empowering and integrating marginalised, disadvantaged and/or vulnerable groups as well as promoting gender equality into public life. To guarantee human rights and fundamental freedoms for the whole of society, a non-discriminatory approach to policy-making and service provision based on the needs of all societal groups is vital. Applying a **gender equality and inclusiveness lens** in decision-making process, in combination with openness and transparency, can help governments better understand the needs of people of all genders across the broadest of cross-sections of society, and how to respond to them more effectively. Such a lens also helps decision-makers assess the differentiated impacts of their decisions - across policy themes or sectors - on people of all genders from different backgrounds, to evaluate whether any given policy mitigates or reinforces existing inequalities. Governments pursue inclusiveness by leveraging the information, ideas and resources held by all stakeholders, including citizens, civil society organisations and the private sector, and by better engaging with them in tailoring policies and services to societal needs.

Vulnerable societal groups of different kinds (e.g. based on religion, ethnicity, language, sexual orientation, age, physical abilities etc.) have traditionally been underrepresented in policy-making processes. In order to guarantee inclusiveness, gender equality and diversity policymakers should ensure that engagement with the whole of society is mainstreamed across the government and that specific measures are implemented to ensure the targeted participation of all societal groups. **Youth** is an additional key actor for improving diversity in policy-making. While all age groups' needs and interests should be equally considered in policy-making for the sake of intergenerational equity, it is often the young generation that is the least politically organised and represented. With young men and women politically empowered and more actively engaged in policy-making, societies can be more cohesive and resilient, and democracies more vibrant. However, according to the OECD Youth Stocktaking Report (2018[24]), in 17 out of 30 OECD Member countries for which data exists, youth express less trust in government than their parents (aged 50+) and their participation in formal processes appears to be on the decline.

Three main enablers to increase inclusiveness, gender equality and diversity in governance are listed here: the first one has to do with strong institutional mechanisms, tools and accountability structures; the second one with effective stakeholder participation and the third one ensure gender equality, diversity and inclusiveness in decision-making positions.

**Regarding strong institutional mechanisms, tools and accountability structures.** In this regard, the *OECD Recommendation on Gender Equality in Public Life* (2015[25]) [OECD/LEGAL/0418] provides important guidance in this regard which can be applied to all inclusiveness approaches:

- **Adopting a "whole-of-state" governance approach** to gender and broader equality mainstreaming: the *Recommendation on Gender Equality in Public Life* proposes a system-wide approach which recognises that all public institutions and branches of the state have a strong role to play in promoting gender equality and inclusiveness. The Centre of Government (CoG) can play a critical role as the "power house" influencing change across the system.

- **Leveraging all core government decision-making tools** to promote inclusiveness and gender equality: All ministries and government agencies can integrate evidence-based assessments of impact on politically underrepresented and/or marginalised groups and considerations into various dimensions of public governance and in the early stages of all phases of the policy cycle. Decision-makers can also consider integration of the inclusiveness, equity, gender, etc. perspective in all phases of the budget cycle so that transparency regarding gender-relevant resource allocation decisions is maximised.

  o For instance, several countries has launched national youth policies/strategies to unite ministries, different levels of government and non-governmental stakeholders around a joint vision that delivers youth-related policies and services in a coherent manner with the active participation of young people. Moreover, countries can implement youth checks, which assess the expected impact of new regulations on young men and women and hence broaden the default "adult" perspective in regulatory policy-making.

  o **Strengthening accountability and oversight mechanisms** for gender equality and inclusiveness mainstreaming initiatives across and within government bodies (Box 1.8).

---

**Box 1.8. Sweden's Programme for Gender Mainstreaming in Government Agencies (GMGA)**

To achieve gender equality policy objectives, the Swedish government launched a Nationwide Government Programme for Gender Mainstreaming in Government Agencies (GMGA) 2012-2019. The programme encompasses sixty agencies in the cultural, judiciary, labour and health care sectors. These agencies must integrate a gender equality perspective in their core activities, following a tailor-made action plan.

Reports from the Swedish Gender Equality Agency and the mid-term evaluation from the Swedish Agency for Public management indicate that agencies have identified critical challenges as well positive results linked to their contribution to gender equality. In light of these results, the Government recently expanded the programme to over 30 higher education institutions and implemented similar programmes to promote LGBT Rights and the Rights of the Child.

Source: Example of country practice provided by the Government of Sweden as part of the Policy Framework's consultation process

---

**A second key enabler** of inclusive governance is **effective stakeholder participation**. Actively engaging stakeholders contributes to the well-targeted use of limited state resources and better public service design and delivery, for example through consulting citizens for the identification of their needs. Active participation goes beyond votes and elections and recognises the capacity of citizens to co-generate policy options (OECD, 2016[23]). Stakeholder participation – one of the open government principles - increases government inclusiveness and accountability, broadens citizen empowerment and influence on decisions and builds civic capacity. Stakeholder participation "improves the evidence base for policy-making, reduces implementation costs and taps wider network for innovation in policy-making and service delivery" (OECD, 2009[26]).

The *OECD Recommendation on Open Government* (2017[22]) [OECD/LEGAL/0438] advises governments "to grant all stakeholders equal and fair opportunities to be informed and consulted and actively engage them in all phases of the policy-cycle and service design and delivery". Governments should, moreover, "promote innovative ways to effectively engage with stakeholders to source ideas and co-create solutions and seize the opportunities provided by digital government tools, including through the use of open government data". The Recommendation also includes an inclusive definition of stakeholders as "any interested and/or affected party, including: individuals, regardless of their age, gender, sexual orientation, religious and political affiliations; and institutions and organisations, whether governmental or non-governmental, from civil society, academia, the media or the private sector".

In that regard, the *OECD Recommendation on Digital Government Strategies* (OECD, 2014[31]) [OECD/LEGAL/0406] recommends governments to develop and implement digital government strategies that encourage engagement and participation of public, private and civil society stakeholders in policy-making and public service design and delivery. OECD Member countries have developed different initiatives; inter alia, improved arrangements for civic and citizenship education, online consultations, the strategic use of social media and more traditional initiatives such as the establishment of interest groups/institutions.

Moreover, as it will be observed in chapters 3 and 4, stakeholder engagement is a key component of a sound regulatory policy. The *OECD Recommendation on Regulatory Policy and Governance* (2012[27]) [OECD/LEGAL/0390] suggest that governments "establish a clear policy identifying how open and balanced public consultation on the development of rules will take place" (OECD, 2012[27]). In this regard, and as is the case for integrity and openness frameworks, best practice identified by the OECD on stakeholder engagement in regulatory policy includes:

- A clear, crosscutting, government-wide guiding policy should exist on how to engage with stakeholders, setting clear objectives.
- Leadership and strong commitment to stakeholder engagement in regulation-making are needed at all levels, from politicians, senior managers and public officials.
- Capacities in public administration to conduct effective and efficient stakeholder engagement should receive adequate attention.
- Mechanisms to ensure that civil servants adhere to the principles of open government and stakeholder engagement in regulatory policy.

While many countries are making important progress in the design and implementation of participatory initiatives, data shows that their full potential is not yet being achieved, especially during the final phases of the policy cycle. As for open government strategies, the development of specific policy and legislative frameworks for greater inclusiveness should favour the use of participatory practices at all points in the policy-making cycle by defining which mechanisms to use and how stakeholder participation should be encouraged at each stage. Making the business case for effective engagement - measuring the cost associated with such exercises and their final impact - will also be essential for improving the strategic use of citizen-participation practices.

**A third important element** to build inclusiveness is to ensure gender equality, diversity and inclusiveness in **decision-making positions**. The OECD recognises that "fostering gender diversity and inclusion, including gender diversity in public decision-making is critical for achieving inclusive growth at all levels of government, as well as anticipating current and future steps needed to increase citizen trust and well-being" (OECD, 2015[25]). Yet women still make up for only one third of leadership positions across all three branches of power. Moving forward, the *OECD Recommendation on Gender Equality in Public Life* (2015[25]) [OECD/LEGAL/0418] provides guidance to countries on how to achieve gender balanced representation in decision-making positions in public life, and improve the gender equality in public employment, including at the top. Moreover, there is increasing recognition that all societal groups should be represented adequately in elected bodies, the government cabinet and the public administration to embrace their innovative potential and deliver on the needs of all.

## Core questions for consideration

- Have you identified government-wide objectives to mainstream inclusiveness across the public sector? Are these objectives supported by governance and performance strategies? Are they integrated into government-wide policy objectives and priorities?
- Is there a whole-of-government institutional framework in place, with clear roles and responsibilities assigned for the centre of government, institutions responsible for gender equality, all line ministries and agencies and oversight institutions (e.g. the Ombudsperson) – accompanied by sufficient resources, adequate capacities and coordination structures – to systematically embed and oversee the implementation of gender equality and an inclusiveness lens in decision-making?
- Is gender-disaggregated data and information – including information on intersectionality factors available and used to inform decision-making?
- Is disaggregated data and information available for vulnerable societal groups and are these resources used to inform decision-making?
- Are policies, mechanisms and tools in place to promote gender-balanced and inclusive participation in decision-making and leadership in the public sector?[2]

## Accountability, and the respect for the Rule of Law

Public accountability constitutes a key element for governments and public institutions to ensure the efficiency and effectiveness of the machinery of government and, more generally, to strengthen citizens' trust in the institutions of government. Nowadays, the whole public sector is facing increased pressure to deliver more with less and to show to citizens how their money is being spent. In many countries, public accountability is not the sole responsibility of one organ or public entity but of many institutions. Public officials must ensure that government activities and decisions respond to citizens' needs and demands. Horizontal accountability ensures that the different branches of the state, namely the executive, the legislative, the judiciary, as well as independent institutions (ombudsman, supreme audit institutions, and special commissions) hold each other accountable on behalf of the people. While public accountability is certainly pivotal at the national level, it is also of particular importance at subnational levels where citizens and policies meet: local governments are responsible for the most tangible and basic public services.

The proximity between elected officials and citizens at the local level creates informal mechanisms favouring vertical accountability, which refers to the direct relationship between on the one hand, citizens, media, and civil society organizations and, on the other hand, their elected and non-elected public officials. The widespread use of digital technologies, coupled with improved internet penetration worldwide, the increasing presence of politicians and public institutions on social media, the open government movement and the diffusion of the principles and practices of transparency and stakeholders' participation – these are all reshaping the legal, institutional, governance and policy frameworks as we have known them to date.

Accountability lines, which in their most simplistic form can be defined as "who does what and reports to whom", become blurry and dynamic, as they change from country to country as well as across political cycles. Once clearly identifiable and legally enforced, nowadays the responsibilities of politicians, public officials and citizens are undergoing a profound transformation which requires a rethinking of the ways in which formal traditional accountability (State, administrative and financial) should be integrated with more citizen's-centred accountability and interactive bottom-up practices (i.e. citizen journalism or open data initiatives).

---

### Box 1.9. Types of accountability

- State accountability: Frameworks that ensure that public institutions hold each other to account on behalf of the people and that check and balances are respected in the country including mechanisms in the Executive, the Legislative (i.e. its oversight role through commissions, investigative powers, question time, etc.) and the Judicial branches, as well as the role of independent institutions such as the Ombudsman, ad hoc commissions, Supreme Audit Institutions or supranational entities, among others.

- Administrative accountability: A robust system of internal control ensures that institutions and public servants are carrying out tasks according to agreed performance criteria, using mechanisms that reduce abuse, improve adherence to standards and foster learning for improved performance including country's internal control system in order to be strategic, preventive and to advance risk management to ensure administrative accountability and detect inefficiencies that can affect the efficiency and effectiveness of public institutions.

- Financial accountability: Budgetary governance is the process of formulating the annual budget, overseeing its implementation and ensuring its alignment with public goals. Ensuring accountability throughout the budget cycle can potentially contribute to more efficient and effective service delivery.

- Social accountability: Ensuring that the voices of people are being heard and acknowledging that the role of citizens in policymaking has transformed the relationship governments-citizenry is key for governments to restore citizens' trust including the possibility to hold free, fair and transparent elections and the country's party system, the existence of citizen engagement practices, the social capital, the role of CSOs and the level of transparency and access to public information as well as the role of media and journalism to hold government accountable, to act as watchdogs and as a means to provide information.

- Policy outcome accountability: Policymakers account for their performance by monitoring and evaluating policy outcomes and making available relevant performance information in a timely manner. As policymakers are held accountable, there is an opportunity to learn from the past while fostering greater reliance on evidence-informed policy-making.

---

**The rule of law represents a core element for accountability and one of the foundational values defining the like-mindedness of OECD Member countries**. It is intertwined with the other governance dimensions of accountability, transparency, openness and integrity, and defines these dimensions' interdependence. Sustainable Development Goal (SDG) 16.3 calls on countries to "promote the rule of law at the national and international levels, and ensure equal access to justice for all".

**Effective and efficient justice systems are crucial to sustaining the rule of law and sound public governance - notably of policy and regulatory performance.** For instance, effective anti-corruption efforts depend on sound and accessible justice institutions at all levels of government within a framework that guarantees that every last individual in society is equal under the law and that no individual or group obtains special treatment under the law by virtue of origin or background, socio-economic circumstances or links to society's power structures.

*Constitutional justice* performs important functions in the consolidation and maintenance of democratic governments by guaranteeing the protection of individual rights and liberties, establishing the separation of powers between government branches and bodies, and enabling capacity for dialogue between the people and their government.

*Administrative justice* is one of the main interfaces between public administration and people. For example, the *Recommendation on Regulatory Policy and Governance* (OECD, 2012[27]) [OECD/LEGAL/0390] highlights that judicial review constitutes a litmus test of good regulatory practice by:

- ensuring that regulators exercise authority within the scope of their legal powers
- providing an incentive for regulators to adhere to good governance and best practice principles
- protecting regulators from undue influences from government
- enhancing trust and legitimacy of regulatory activity as part of economic policy agenda

**Access to - and satisfaction with - justice services are important contributors to, and drivers of, trust in government.** Access to justice and legal empowerment are important tools to advance the open government and open state agenda as they are drivers of social accountability, public-sector integrity and inclusive growth. Legal empowerment advances more meaningful civic engagement by ensuring that people understand how the law allows them not only to confront injustice in their lives but to participate in law-making and the implementation of legislation for society's benefit.

A sound and functioning legal and justice system contributes to a thriving business environment and longer-term investment decisions. It supports contract enforcement, reduces transaction costs and levels the playing field for market stakeholders by instilling confidence in "the rules of the game," ensuring fair competition and protecting property rights. The *OECD Policy Framework for Investment (PFI)* highlights that when key elements of effective access to justice are missing or inefficient (e.g. complex, costly, and lengthy procedures), companies including SMEs tend to limit their activities in that jurisdiction/country (OECD, 2015[28]).

**Access to justice lies at the centre of inclusive growth strategies** aimed at improving policy outcomes. Lack of legal empowerment and unequal access to justice through e.g. high procedural costs and significant waiting times, generate significant socio-economic costs for individuals and societies. Access to justice engenders equality of access to opportunities and public services. According to the OECD Framework for Policy Action on Inclusive Growth (2018[29]), it is a key building block for enabling stakeholders to "invest in people and places that have been left behind".

People's unmet legal and justice needs (e.g. family, racial, employment, housing, violence against women, consumer-related) can have adverse effects on other areas of everyday life, e.g. health, social welfare and economic well-being. Conversely, direct and indirect benefits are attributable to meeting particular legal needs and providing legal assistance and access-to-justice programmes, notably in such areas as better housing, supporting inclusion, enhancing consumer and financial protection reducing domestic or family violence and facilitating access to healthcare (Box 1.10).

---

Colombia has made important advances in its efforts to measure and map the legal needs of its population through the use of a comprehensive legal needs survey. This component was introduced in the Quality of Life Survey conducted by the National Department of Statistics and the National Planning Department of Colombia in 2016. It builds on methodologies and experiences of the civil society organisation Dejusticia, which had previously conducted an urban legal needs survey in Colombia.

Based on the survey results, Colombia developed the Effective Access to Justice Index to inform their long-term justice plan. It helps to measure and compare the capacity of Colombia's regions and departments to provide effective access to justice. It explores six dimensions of access to justice:

- favourable environment (which is concerned with structural and institutional barriers to justice that lie outside of the justice system);
- legal capability;
- legal assistance;
- fair procedure;
- compliance with judicial decisions; and
- access to institutions.

Colombia is currently preparing the next legal needs survey to be carried out in 2020 as a module of the Citizenship Security Survey. It will aim to collect data at the national and regional level (both urban and rural areas), including several main cities.

Source: OECD (2019[76]), Equal Access to Justice for Inclusive Growth: Putting People at the Centre, OECD Publishing, Paris, https://doi.org/10.1787/597f5b7f-en; OECD/Open Society Foundations (2019[77]), Legal Needs Surveys and Access to Justice, OECD Publishing, Paris, https://doi.org/10.1787/g2g9a36c-en ; Information provided by the National Planning Department of Colombia.

---

One of the most important trends in OECD Member countries is the shift towards **people-centred justice** as a guiding principle, which implies adopting clear and easy understandable language so that citizens can understand laws and legal documents as well as providing access to legal and justice services from the individual's perspective and experience. It acknowledges that specific groups, notably the disadvantaged, may have additional legal needs and face extra barriers in accessing justice services.

Effective access to legal and justice services presupposes an enabling framework for an effective and efficient justice system. Such frameworks encompass a growing spectrum (or "continuum") of services, processes and procedures, and tend to include a legal architecture, institutional arrangements and alternative dispute-resolution mechanisms (specialised mediation services; problem-solving courts; justice-access centres; etc.), strategic planning and performance management, data system exchanges, monitoring and evaluation systems, sound HR provisions related to the professional career (judicial and non-judicial), among other things. Indeed acknowledging the relationship between effective access to justice and broader socio-economic outcomes has prompted countries to co-ordinate justice and social services under an outcome-based approach, i.e. addressing both people's justice needs and their accompanying social or health issues (e.g., domestic violence, drug and alcohol abuse, mental illness, juvenile delinquency).

Evidence of good practice of OECD Members and Partners shows that designing and delivering people-focused legal and justice services require a coherent approach shaped by effective coordination across strategic priority areas optimising the use of available resources in a way that best reflects the specific political, socioeconomic and service environment of the country. This approach calls for:

- *the systematic identification, measurement and mapping of legal needs,* to help determine who experiences legal needs where (at the national, sub-national and local levels), along with the nature and scope of these needs. A number of OECD Member countries are using legal needs survey methodologies – in combination with different types of administrative data – to allow policymakers to understand the actual scope of legal needs and people's pathways to resolving them.

- *designing and delivering people-centred legal and justice services,* to effectively respond in a targeted and fair manner to identified legal needs. Practice in OECD Member countries suggests that legal and justice services are people-centric and effective when they are provided in an inclusive manner and available both to the general population and specific vulnerable groups, are effectively responsive; help build empowerment; prioritise proactivity, prevention and timeliness; and focus on substantive outcomes.

- *adopting a data-driven approach* to identify measures of demand, supply and outcomes. This helps deliver justice services in a manner that can optimise the relative costs of different strategies, identify alternative financing possibilities to achieving a desired outcome for specific groups of the population and ensure that justice services generate value for money. Several evaluation methods (such as cost-effectiveness, cost-benefit analysis, economic impact analysis) can be used for this purpose.

**Figure 1.3. Planning for Effective Access to Justice: What works practices in designing and delivering**

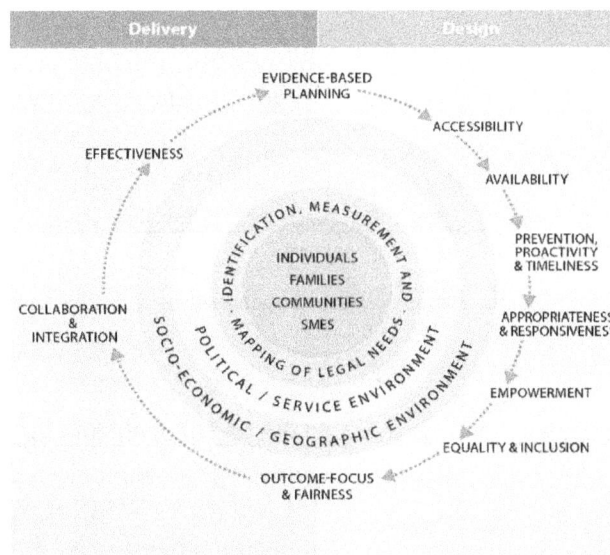

*Source*: OECD (2019), Equal Access to Justice for Inclusive Growth: Putting People at the Centre, OECD Publishing, Paris, https://doi.org/10.1787/597f5b7f-en.

## Core questions for consideration

- What mechanisms are in place to ensure that public institutions hold each other to account on behalf of the people and that check and balances are respected in the country?

- What mechanisms are in place promote and protect the existence of stakeholders engagement practices, including those for citizens, CSOs and media to hold government accountable?

- Is there a systematic process for mapping legal needs and experience to understand if and how appropriate types of services are being matched to the needs of different groups of population across all regions in the country?

- Are there effective coordination and communication channels vertically (across levels of government) and horizontally (between various legal and justice services including courts) to support governance and alignment in justice services?

- Is there a data management or exchange system covering formal and non-formal legal and justice services and based on common data protocols and standards? Is this information readily available to the public?

## Additional resources

OECD legal instruments:

- OECD Recommendation of the Council on Public Integrity (2017) [OECD/LEGAL/0435]
- OECD Recommendation of the Council on Guidelines for Managing Conflict of Interest in the Public Service (2003) [OECD/LEGAL/0316]
- OECD Recommendation of the Council on Principles for Transparency and Integrity in Lobbying (2010) [OECD/LEGAL/0379]
- OECD Recommendation of the Council for Further Combating Bribery of Foreign Public Officials (2009) [OECD/LEGAL/0378]
- OECD Recommendation of the Council on Open Government (2017) [OECD/LEGAL/0438]
- OECD Recommendation of the Council on Gender Equality in Public Life (2015) [OECD/LEGAL/0418]
- OECD Recommendation of the Council on Open Government (2017) [OECD/LEGAL/0438]
- OECD Recommendation of the Council on Digital Government Strategies (2014) [OECD/LEGAL/0406]
- OECD Recommendation of the Council on Regulatory policy and Governance (2012) [OECD/LEGAL/0390]

Other relevant OECD tools:

- G20/OECD Compendium of good practices on the use of open data for Anti-corruption (2017)
- Behavioural Insights for Public Integrity - Harnessing the Human Factor to Counter Corruption (2018)
- Education for Integrity - Teaching on Anti-Corruption, Values and the Rule of Law (2018)
- Government at a Glance (2017)
- Integrity Framework for Public Investment (2016)
- Investing in Integrity for Productivity (2016)
- Financing Democracy - Funding of Political Parties and Election Campaigns and the Risk of Policy Capture (2016)
- Supreme Audit Institutions and Good Governance: Oversight, Insight and Foresight (2016)
- Lobbyists, Governments and Public Trust, Volume 3: Implementing the OECD Principles for Transparency and Integrity in Lobbying (2014)
- Managing Conflict of Interest in the Public Sector - A Toolkit (2005)

- OECD Open Government: The Global Context and the Way Forward (2016)
- Citizens as Partners: OECD Handbook on Information, Consultation and Public Participation in Policy-Making (2001)
- OECD Toolkit for Implementing and Mainstreaming Gender Equality (2018)
- OECD Best Practice Principles on Stakeholder Engagement in Regulatory Policy (forthcoming)
- OECD Youth Stocktaking Report (2018) OECD Youth Stocktaking Report (2018)
- Citizens as Partners: OECD Handbook on Information, Consultation and Public Participation in Policy-Making (2001)
- OECD Recommendation of the Council on Gender Equality in Public Life (2015)
- Opportunities for All: A Framework for Policy Action on Inclusive Growth, OECD Publishing, Paris (2018)
- OECD-Open Society Foundations Guide on Legal Needs Surveys and Access to Justice, OECD Publishing, Paris (2019)
- OECD White Paper: Building a Business Case for Access to Justice (2019)

## References

Agency for Modernisation, Local Government Denmark and Danish Regions (2017), *Code of conduct in the Public Sector*.  [15]

Denmark Ministry of Finance (2015), *Seven key duties for civil servants in central government*- http://www.modst.dk/kodexvii (accessed on 4 October 2019).  [16]

Mor, F. (2019), "Registers of beneficial ownership", House of Commons Library Briefing Paper No 8259, London: House of commons library, https://researchbriefings.files.parliament.uk/documents/CBP-8259/CBP-8259.pdf  [21]

Murtin, F. et al. (2018), "Trust and its determinants: Evidence from the Trustlab experiment", *OECD Statistics Working Papers*, No. 2018/2, OECD Publishing, Paris, https://dx.doi.org/10.1787/869ef2ec-en.  [8]

OECD (2019), *Recommendation of the Council on Public Service Leadership and Capability*.  [9]

OECD (2019), *Equal Access to Justice for Inclusive Growth: Putting People at the Centre*, OECD Publishing, Paris, https://dx.doi.org/10.1787/597f5b7f-en.  [76]

OECD (2018), *Opportunities for All: A Framework for Policy Action on Inclusive Growth*, OECD Publishing, Paris, https://dx.doi.org/10.1787/9789264301665-en.  [29]

OECD (2018), *Behavioural Insights for Public Integrity: Harnessing the Human Factor to Counter Corruption*, OECD Public Governance Reviews, OECD Publishing, Paris, https://dx.doi.org/10.1787/9789264297067-en.  [14]

OECD (2018), *Education for Integrity Teaching on Anti-Corruption, Values and the Rule of Law*, OECD Publishing, Paris.  [17]

OECD (2018), Youth Stocktaking Report, OECD Publishing, Paris.  [24]

OECD (2017), Recommendation of the Council on Open Government, [OECD/LEGAL/0438].  [22]

OECD (2017), *Recommendation of the Council on Public Integrity*.  [11]

OECD (2017), *Trust and Public Policy: How Better Governance Can Help Rebuild Public Trust*, OECD Public Governance Reviews, OECD Publishing, Paris, https://dx.doi.org/10.1787/9789264268920-en. [7]

OECD (2016), *Supreme Audit Institutions and Good Governance: Oversight, Insight and Foresight*, OECD Public Governance Reviews, OECD Publishing, Paris, https://dx.doi.org/10.1787/9789264263871-en. [18]

OECD (2016), Open Government:The global context and the way forward, OECD Publishing, Paris. [23]

OECD (2015), *Policy Framework for Investment,* OECD Publishing, Paris, https://dx.doi.org/10.1787/9789264208667-en. [28]

OECD (2015), Recommendation of the Council on Gender Equality in Public Life, [OECD/LEGAL/0418]. [25]

OECD (2014), Recommendation of the Council on Digital Government Strategies, [OECD/LEGAL/0406]. [31]

OECD (2012), *Recommendation of the Council on Regulatory Policy and Governance* [27]

OECD (2010), *Recommendation of the Council on Transparency and Integrity in Lobbying.* [19]

OECD (2009), *Recommendation of the Council for Further Combating Bribery of Foreign Public Officials in International Business Transactions.* [12]

OECD (2009), Focus on Citizens: Public Engagement for Better Policy and Services, OECD Studies on Public Engagement, OECD Publishing, Paris, https://dx.doi.org/10.1787/9789264048874-en. [26]

OECD (2003), *Managing Conflict of Interest in the Public Service: OECD Guidelines and Country Experiences*, OECD Publishing, Paris. [20]

OECD/Open Society Foundations (2019), *Legal Needs Surveys and Access to Justice*, OECD Publishing, Paris, https://dx.doi.org/10.1787/g2g9a36c-en. [77]

Schickora, J., V. Fakultät and J. Schikora (2011), *Bringing the Four-Eyes-Principle to the Lab*, Discussion Papers in Economics 2011:3. [13]

# 2 The Enablers of Sound Public Governance

This chapter discusses a key set of enablers that, along with governance values, can contribute to effective governance and a better definition as well as implementation of policy and governance reforms across government. The chapter identifies four enablers, namely: commitment, vision and leadership; equitable and evidence-informed policy-making; whole-of-government co-ordination; as well as change management and innovation. In all likelihood, no policy or reform initiative make use of these practices in a flawless and integrated way, nevertheless this chapter argues that adopting them can contribute to substantive changes in the way governments make decisions and address reforms.

At the same time as public-policy challenges have become more complex and multidimensional, they have become more interconnected through globalisation and greater interdependence among nations. Climate change, migration, inequality: challenges are now characterised by rising uncertainty, increasing complexity, interdependent processes, structures and actors. In this unpredictable context, governments are facing pressure to design and deliver better policies and services, while simultaneously grappling with unprecedented fiscal-stabilisation challenges and trust levels below those that followed the 2008 financial crisis. Trust is difficult to rebuild when governments face the perception that reforms are ineffective and do not sufficiently take into account the needs of losers in the context of the gains of winners (OECD, 2017[1]).

Lessons learned from OECD experience in supporting policy and public-governance reform efforts of Members and Partners suggest that governments are facing the general perception that reform is often seen as a means to save money rather than solve policy challenges. Public governance is a political process, in which the government is not necessary a monolithic decision maker and multiple interests play a role. The way public decisions are made, which information they use and how interests interact behind these decisions define the parameters of policy-making and governance reform. Moreover as interdependence increases, outcomes, trade-offs, and the winners and losers of reform are more difficult to identify, generating considerable additional challenges for successful policy-making.

Governments need to adapt to the new public sector challenges. This might require transforming bureaucracies, institutional arrangements and governance cultures that have been in place for decades (in some cases centuries). Some government are focusing on agility, experimentation, enabling bottom-up innovation, and testing and scaling to deal with complexity and uncertainty, overlapping policy cycles and greater demand for external voices. However, the necessity of new innovative approaches is simultaneous to the necessity of meeting traditional demands of governments in terms of service delivery. In this context, how can governments plan and implement this transformation process? How can citizens and governments be sure that these transformations are driven by a fair willingness to resolve these issues? And how can they tackle complex policy challenges and launch a reform process in a more effective way?

There is no definitive responses to these questions. Countries are still exploring new mechanisms to deal with complexity and civil society. In parallel, citizens still demand more effective means of representation and participation. Nevertheless, key practices have been adopted by countries to approach reform and transformation in a more effective way:

- **Leadership**, politically and stemming from of the civil service, is key to promote and drive change through all levels of the public administration and beyond. Moreover, reforms tend to be more effective when they contribute to the realisation of a common **vision**, to the common interest and do not constitute isolated efforts which perpetuate the same winners and losers (OECD, 2014[30]).

- Reforms tend to work best when they are the subject of sustained **commitment** from the highest political and management levels to ensure their effective implementation and sustainability.

- Public decision-making should aim to be equitable and driven at all times by a commitment to serve the public interest. To this end, evidence-informed decision-making can play a key role in improving the design, implementation and evaluation of public policies. This also means government should proactively seek the views of stakeholders at all key points in the policy cycle, as highlighted in chapter 1, to optimise the state's accountability, responsiveness and integrity.

- An integrated and innovative approach to reform requires overcoming traditional administrative barriers to designing, implementing and evaluating the performance of multidimensional policy responses through robust, sustained **whole-of-government coordination** across policy areas, administrative silos within governments, and between levels of government.

- Successful reforms also place high political and institutional priority to **innovation and experimentation to manage change successfully** over time, in order to create more agile and responsive institutions.

In all likelihood, no policy or reform initiative make use of these practices in a flawless and integrated way. Policymakers usually deal with day-to-day emergencies that leave little room for effective co-ordination meetings, for experimentation or the development of innovation approaches or for sustained stakeholder engagement. Nevertheless adopting these practices in a progressive way can contribute to substantive changes in the way governments approach change. Future editions of the Framework will aim to propose more tailored sequential guidance and advice on reform enablers, for instance through implementation toolkits and maturity models.

## Figure 2.1. The Enablers of Reform and of Sound Public Governance

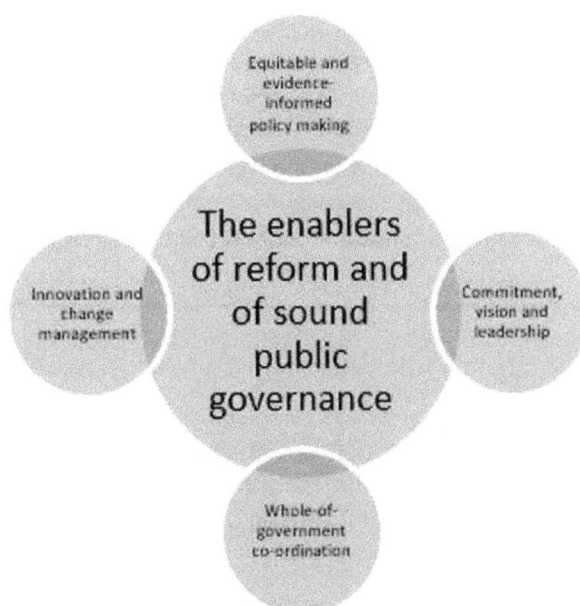

*Source: Authors' own elaboration.*

## Commitment, vision and leadership

**Commitment** at the highest political level appropriate to the scale of reform being undertaken, is crucial to ensuring the success of reforms. Without commitment to reform from the highest political level, for public service leadership struggles to find incentives to pursue medium-term reform initiatives as it goes about managing its day-to-day responsibilities while fixing short-term, urgent issues.

Governments can exercise leadership in this area by expressing a strong political commitment for better governance and demonstrating the political will to endorse and recommends this approach in areas such as regulation, gender equality in public life, digital government and integrity:

- *The Recommendation on Regulatory Policy and Governance* [OECD/LEGAL/0390] recommends that Adherents commit at the highest political level to an explicit whole-of-government policy for regulatory quality (OECD, 2012[27]).
- *The Recommendation on Gender Equality in Public Life* [OECD/LEGAL/0418] suggests that Adherents secure leadership and commitment at the highest political level as well as at the appropriate level of government in order to develop and implement a whole-of government strategy for effective gender equality and mainstreaming (OECD, 2015[25]).

- *The Recommendation on Digital Government Strategies* [OECD/LEGAL/0406] recommends that Adherents secure leadership and political commitment for the strategy, through a combination of efforts aimed at promoting inter-ministerial co-ordination and collaboration, setting priorities and facilitate engagement and co-ordination of relevant agencies across levels of government in pursuing the digital government agenda. (OECD, 2014[31])

- *The Recommendation on Public Integrity* [OECD/LEGAL/0435] recommends that Adherents demonstrate commitment at the highest political and management levels within the public sector to enhance public integrity and reduce corruption (2017[11]).

The **Centre of Government** (CoG) (Box 2.1) can play an important role in mainstreaming reform across the public administration. In OECD Member countries, the CoG is playing an increasingly important role in driving strategic priorities, closely linked with their increasing responsibilities on policy co-ordination (see Section 2.3.). According to the *OECD Survey on the Organisation and Functions of Centres of Government*, and its report *Centre Stage*, the CoG tends to play a prominent role in temporarily driving sensitive and/or structural reforms of the public administration, in particular at their initial stage (OECD, 2018[32]). This temporary assignment can send a strong message of political commitment both within the public sector and to the public. This has been the case in a number of OECD countries with e-government strategies and with red tape/administrative burden reduction initiatives (OECD, 2014[33]).

---

### Box 2.1. What is the Centre of Government?

The strategic role of Centre of Government (CoG) has been expanding over the course of the last decade due to the increasing complexity of policy-making and the emergence of whole-of-government strategy-setting and implementation, strategic monitoring of government performance over the medium term, and strategic issues management.

The CoG is "the body of group of bodies that provide direct support and advice to Heads of Government and the Council of Minister, or Cabinet". The CoG is mandated to ensure the consistency and prudency of government decisions and "to promote evidence-based, strategic and consistent policies" (OECD, 2014[33]).

The CoG concept does not make explicit reference to any particular organisational structure: institutions vary from one country to another, depending on the constitutional order, the political system, the administrative structure of the country, contextual and historical actors and even the personality of the chief executive. Therefore, expanded definitions of the CoG can include institutions or agencies which perform core cross-cutting governmental functions, such as finance or planning ministries, even if they are not reporting directly to, or supporting, the Head of Government/Head of State and Council of Ministers.

Source: OECD(2014[33]) Centre Stage, Driving Better Policies from the Centre of Government, https://www.oecd.org/gov/Centre-Stage-Report.pdf ; Alessandro, M, et al. (Alessandro, Lafuente and Santiso, 2013[34]) The Role of the Center of Government: a Literature Review, Institutions for Development, Technical Note, IDB-TN-581, IDB, Washington, DC, https://publications.iadb.org/handle/11319/5988

---

A broad government commitment can usually find expression in a government **vision**. As shown in the *Centre Stage* report on driving better policies from the CoG, nearly all OECD Member countries have some sort of strategic vision document. In this regard, OECD experience garnered through its country reviews has shown that governments can give better coherence to the activities when they have the capacity to define, implement and communicate both internally and externally their strategic visions, a means to orient the state, civil society, the private sector and citizens toward a common goal (OECD, 2011[78]).

How this vision is formulated and translated into specific long or medium-term strategies and policy decisions is an important process as it contributes to defining priorities and objectives along with the nature and scope of reforms; it underpins the rationale for better coordination as a means to pursue it. Strategic foresight, horizon scanning and debates on alternative futures with stakeholders are different tools that can support governments in the elaboration of a vision that incorporates trends and possible scenarios. A vision-building exercise and planning process that are open and include robust stakeholder engagement can legitimise policy-making and can constitute an effective tool to ensure the sustainability of reforms (OECD, 2016[23])

In this connection, **public service leadership** is also fundamental to achieve successful reforms for sound public governance. Public service leadership refers to senior-level public servants, who are those public servants who take decisions and exert influence at the highest hierarchical levels of the professional public service. In today's complex political and policy environment, senior-level public servants are expected to work effectively across administrative and policy silos, responding diligently and ethically to support rapidly changing political agendas and reacting with agility to unpredictable developments. As senior-level public servants usually link strategy to policy execution, governments should invest in building a values-driven culture and leadership in the public service, centred on improving outcomes for society. Senior-management leadership can help ensure the effective policy design and implementation by drawing from institutional knowledge and experience to contribute to evidence-based decision-making[3]. Investing in leadership is an important catalyser for effective reform, regardless of the area or policy theme. This includes building effective systems for competitive and merit-based appointments of senior management and heads of agencies.

Recognising the essential role of these key actors, the *OECD Recommendation on Public Service leadership and Capability* (2019[9]) [OECD/LEGAL/0445] specifically recommends Adherents build leadership capability in the public service. The guidance it provides encourages governments to:

- Clarify the expectations incumbent upon senior-level public servants to be politically impartial leaders of public organisations, trusted to deliver on the priorities of the government, and uphold and embody the highest standards of integrity without fear of politically-motivated retribution. This suggests the need to codify these expectations in law and ensure they are upheld and regularly monitored. Similarly, conflict of interest issues should be systematically reported and addressed though clear procedures.

- Select and appoint the right people to these positions considering merit-based criteria and transparent procedures, and holding them accountable for performance through appropriate means. This suggests the need to look at performance management mechanisms for leaders and the integration of these mechanisms into the governance system.

- Ensure senior-level public servants have the mandate, competencies, and conditions necessary to provide impartial evidence-informed advice and speak truth to power.

- Develop the leadership capabilities of current and potential senior-level public servants.

- The *OECD Recommendation on Public Integrity* (2017[11]) [OECD/LEGAL/0435] also suggests investing in integrity leadership to demonstrate a public sector organisation's commitment to integrity.

## Core questions for consideration

- When identifying and pursuing a priority reform initiative, does the government demonstrate sustainable commitment at the highest political and management levels through an explicit institutional measure?

- How can the administration support the government in conveying this commitment towards sound public governance internally within and outside the administration?

- Has the government established a medium to long-term vision and goals, and clear institutional mandates and financial resources for their accomplishment?

- Is there an emphasis put on leadership to support the management of individual and collective performance? Does the government invest in skills to build leadership capability in the public service?

- Does your government use cross-silo coordination instruments or mechanisms to secure alignment of actions and decisions of individual parts of the administration with the government's main objectives, thereby ensuring greater coherence in government action?

## Equitable and evidence-informed policy-making

Policy-making is not the same as technical decision-making. The first typically involves a trade-off between competing social values and different interests (Parkhurst, 2017[35]). Yet managing policy and technical decision-making effectively and efficiently in the general public interest lies at the core of sound public governance. How public decisions are made, which interests lie behind these decisions and what their goals are define the parameters within which reforms leading to sound public governance are designed and carried out. Despite the different features and dynamics of political systems, public decision-making should be framed at all times by the commitment to pursue the public interest – hence the notion of **equitable policy-making**.

When there is a lack of transparency and integrity in decision-making processes, lobbying and other practices to seek influence can be used to steer public policies away from the public interest. Powerful interests can put enormous pressure on government decision-making, determining how and for who our society works. As a result, policies are biased and suboptimal, and real progress towards addressing key policy challenges equitably in the public interest is undermined. This can become a major obstacle to achieving the Sustainable Development Goals (SDGs). Preventing these risks requires fixing distorted decision-making.

Therefore, a pivotal element to guaranteeing equitable decision-making is preventing undue influence by vested interests. If governments make decisions favouring a specific interest group or individual at the expense of the public interest, the whole reform process is affected: policies will privilege the few; evidence will no longer be credible and people will lose trust in their institutions. Levelling the playing field can promote broader consensus and more legitimacy to decisions. This means allowing equitable access to the design and implementation of policy, and strengthening the transparency and integrity of policy-making processes. Equitable decision-making is strengthened when a multiplicity of actors, through robust enabling mechanisms and institutional spaces, promote and work collectively and in a representative manner in the public interest. This includes the necessity of strong and representative institutions, for example political parties, trade unions or trade associations, which represent the different interests of the society. Other institutions such as community-based or issue-based organisation can also offset undue influence and level the playing field. It also includes harnessing new media and channels of representation that can reduce the costs and enhance the impact of collective action.

No government is immune from attempts at undue influence. Given the economic and political interests that are at stake, the public arena is always vulnerable to possible hijacking by one or more special-interest groups. This potentially affects one of the basic tenets of democracy - political equality- and can lead to inequitable and vested-interest-based policy-making. Influence from particular interests of individuals or groups may not be illegal; in fact, it is part of the democratic process. However, fundamental issues emerge when everyone does not share the same opportunity to ensure that their interests are taken into account in the policy-making process. This can occur because of:

- Disproportionate pressure and privileged access through lobbying of public officials,
- Excessive financing of political parties and candidates' electoral campaigns,
- Provision of manipulated or fraudulent expertise or technical data,
- Use of personal connections that lead to conflicts of interests.

---

### Box 2.2. What is policy capture?

Policy capture is the process of directing public policy decisions away from the public interest towards the interests of a specific interest group or person. Capture is the opposite of equitable policy-making, and always undermines core democratic values, while usually also resulting in suboptimal public policies The capture of public decisions can be achieved through a wide variety of illegal instruments, such as bribery, but also through legal channels, such as lobbying and financial support to political parties and election campaigns. Undue influence can also be exercised without the direct involvement or knowledge of public decision makers, by manipulating the information provided to them, or establishing close social or emotional ties with them.

Source: OECD (2017[36]), Preventing Policy Capture, Integrity in Public Decision Making, http://www.oecd.org/corruption/preventing-policy-capture-9789264065239-en.htm.

---

**Policy capture** can happen at all stages of the policy cycle. Hence, over the past decades OECD Member countries have implemented different measures to avoid it. Governance structures should include the means to guarantee that policy and reform decisions are made in the most equitable way, including through the development of a culture of integrity, openness, inclusiveness and respect of the rule of law (see Chapter 1), such as by:

- Engaging stakeholders in the decision-making process as early as possible as a key means to level the playing field and generate a broader consensus and more legitimacy regarding public-policy decisions;
- Strengthening the integrity frameworks of representative institutions, including single-interest ones; for instance through specific regulations that frame their representativeness from a public-integrity standpoint;
- Ensuring strategic communication, transparency and access to complete and updated information to enable civil society and all stakeholders access to the same information, data and evidence when engaging in policy discussions;
- Promoting accountability through competition authorities, regulatory agencies and supreme audit institutions;
- Identifying and mitigating policy-capture risk factors through integrity policies that are tailored to the specifics of different public institutions.

In addition, OECD evidence suggests that countries are adopting key tools to balance stakeholders' ability to influence policymakers against the public interest, including:

- Effective limitations to and oversight over political financing;
- Adequate scrutiny and analysis of policy-making, making this available in an open, transparent and accessible manner to all; and
- Implementing effective controls over lobbying, for instance through the establishment of transparency status for lobbyists and interest managers or the publication of donations taken and trips made by an authority (Box 2.3).

---

**Box 2.3. France's High Authority for transparency in public life**

Since its creation in 2014, France's High Authority for transparency in public life has aimed to uphold the integrity of public officials. Two of the institution's core responsibilities involve promoting probity of French public officials and regulating lobbying:

- Over 15 000 elected officials and civil servants are required to disclose their assets and interests to the High Authority when taking office Since its creation, the institution has received over 42 000 declarations and referred over 60 irregularities to the court. In October 2016, online disclosures became mandatory and some declarations are now published in an open data format following accuracy checks.
- The High Authority also manages an online public register of lobbyists to inform citizens of the relations between lobbyists and decision-makers. Registration is mandatory for firms and associations that seek to influence the decision-making process through interactions with public officials. Over 1 900 entities and 14 000 activities were registered as of July 2019.

Source: Example of country practice provided by the Government of France as part of the Policy Framework's consultation process

---

**The use of evidence in policy-making**; in particular the governance of how evidence is collected, applied and integrated into decision-making on the broad social, political and economic policy challenges of the day, is a key – and complementary – element that can determine the nature and impact of reforms (Parkhurst, 2017[35]). Evidence-informed policy-making can play a critical role in improving the design, implementation and evaluation of all public policies, in ensuring good governance, notably equal access to quality, responsive and people-centred public services.

The collection of evidence can represent a particular challenge for policymakers, specifically in a context where the authority of science in being challenged. Evidence is not always easily available and can present conflicting findings, especially in complex policy areas. Moreover, it is important to assess the credibility and reliability of information, data, and factual evidence (for example through replicability, a multiplicity of sources, independent validation, etc.) used to make decisions. In cases where governmental institutions are not data producers, but consumers, the evidence produced by external actors can be subject to internal assessments of credibility and reliability. Moreover, strong management of the stock of evidence, with robust knowledge-management processes and the full mobilisation of administrative data, will help prevent one-sided policy design, avoid duplication, ensure that scarce resources are directed toward areas of greatest need and that services are designed and delivered based on evidence that demonstrates this need. Governments can lack the capacity to do so, developing skills to commission, understand and use evidence is therefore crucial. This provides the strongest opportunity for designing policies that will benefit citizens, overcome institutional bias and guard against vested interests maintaining the status quo.

While the need for evidence is generally widely accepted, evidence-informed approaches do not obviate the need for political discretion and commitment; they can ensure, however, that all policy choices and trade-offs are fully aired. In a context where the role of social media is growing, with direct access to a range of evidence through web-based channels whose sources are of uneven quality, and with increasing concern for fake news, the need for an evidence-informed approach to decision-making is taking on added importance.

This requires closing the implementation loop from the start, to ensure that the proposed reforms will and can be implemented. Implementation research (including performance evidence) can make a difference between the successful implementation of an intervention and one that is ineffective or even potentially harmful, offering tools for researchers and government officials to monitor the implementation of policies, ensuring they achieve the impacts that policymakers and citizens expect. This requires experimentation, the capacity for policy prototyping and piloting, and appetite, support and capacity for innovation in the public sector.

To close the implementation loop, policy evaluation (Chapter 5) can contribute to identify whether policies are actually improving outcomes. Robust evidence on the efficacy, policy-effectiveness and cost-effectiveness of initiatives ensures that we understand 'what works, why, for whom and under what circumstances'.

Yet experience confirms that reaching this state of affairs is challenging. Even in the most developed systems, challenges in connecting evidence and decision-making remain:

- The civil service needs the right skills to commission, understand and use evidence. This necessitates building capacity at the level of the individual, and supporting the adoption of procedures, incentives and resources to enhance use of evidence.

- Evidence-informed policy-making also requires a supportive institutional set-up and infrastructure with a clear and transparent framework for evidence-generation and use. This might include the existence of quality control and assurance mechanisms to check the reliability and robustness of the evidence collected, before they are actually used.

- Evidence, no matter how robust and relevant, can only ever constitute part of the policy-making process: evidence will always be mediated through a process that integrates intuition and judgement into the shaping of the final policy decision.

Box 2.4. Examples of evidence-informed policy-making initiatives

Capacity building for evidence generation and use – several countries and organisations have made valuable steps to build public sector capacity and use. In the United Kingdom (UK), NESTA with the Alliance for Useful Evidence has created 'Evidence Masterclasses', providing "an immersive learning experience" for senior decision-makers who want to become more skilled and confident users of research.

Evidence Based Clearing Houses and What Works Centres – many OECD Member countries have clearing organisations which systematically review the evidence base underpinning policies and practices, assessing the strength of evidence and communicating this in an easy to understand format. Examples include the California Evidence-Based Clearing House for Child Welfare, the UK What Works Centres, and The Danish Clearinghouse for Educational Research, Kidsmatter Australia and the Swedish Institute for Educational Research.

Source: Authors' own elaboration.

## Core questions for consideration

- Are there mechanisms in place to allow policymakers regularly and proactively engage stakeholders that represent (and disclose) different interests in decision-making processes?
- Does your government have regulations to establish formal and transparent links between interest groups and decision-makers for public decision-making?
- For non-governmental institutions representing specific interests, such as political parties, trade union or trade associations, are there laws or regulations that frame their governance and representativeness from a public-integrity standpoint (as competitive elections for leaders, democratic decision-making; financial transparency and audit requirements; rules respecting electoral financing; etc.)?
- Does the civil service have the knowledge, skills and capacity to ensure a right uptake of quality evidence in policy-making?
- Does the senior civil service have a strategic understanding of the role of evidence-informed policy-making and to ensure that policymakers possess the right evidence at the right time in the right format?
- Does the public sector have the processes and institutional set-up for incorporating evidence in policy-making?
- Is the evidence used by policymakers subject to transparency and integrity requirements? Does the collection of evidence follow particular criteria/requirements to ensure its validity?

## Whole-of-government co-ordination

In recent decades **policy co-ordination** to achieve greater policy coherence has become particularly relevant for many OECD Members and Partners, mainly due to the emergence of cross-cutting, multi-dimensional policy challenges and the subsequent atomisation of administrative structures illustrated by the exponential growth of agencies and other autonomous bodies (Beuselinck, 2008[37]; Alessandro, Lafuente and Santiso, 2013[34]). This is relevant for both horizontal co-ordination across administrative unities (ministries, agencies) as well as vertical co-ordination across level of government (Box 2.5).

Box 2.5. The importance of co-ordination across levels of government

While the initial focus of multi-level governance reforms can be on specific areas, such as infrastructure, OECD experience show that multi-level governance reform should be holistic and multi-dimensional to obviate negative and counterproductive outcomes. Additionally, they should account for regional disparities and develop co-ordination instruments and other management tools to ensure the sustainability. In light of these objectives, the OECD Recommendation of the Council on Effective Public Investment across Levels of Government (2014 ) [OECD/LEGAL/0402] sets out 12 principles grouped into three pillars representing systemic challenges to managing public investment. In particular, the first pillar highlights the importance of co-ordination across governments and policy areas:

- Pillar 1 - Co-ordinate across governments and policy areas, including invest using an integrated strategy tailored to different places; adopt effective co-ordination instrument across levels of government; and co-ordinate across SNGs to invest at the relevant scale
- Pillar 2 - Strengthen capacities and promote policy leaning across levels of government
- Pillar 3 - Ensure sound framework conditions at all levels of government

Source: OECD (2017[38]), Multi-level Governance Reforms: Overview of OECD Country Experiences, OECD Multi-Level Governance Studies, OECD Publishing, Paris, https://doi.org/10.1787/9789264272866-en ; OECD (2019[39]), Effective Public Investment Across Levels of Government: Implementing the OECD Principles, Centre for Entrepreneurship, SMES, Regions and Cities, https://www.oecd.org/effective-public-investment-toolkit/OECD_Principles_For_Action_2019_FINAL.pdf.

Regarding whole-of-government co-ordination, according to *the OECD Survey on Centre of Governments*, most of the countries surveyed (59%) reported that the number of cross-ministerial policy initiatives has grown since 2008 (OECD, 2014[33]). To promote coherence in the way the government works across ministries, agencies and other administrative units, the majority (67%) of OECD Member countries surveyed in the 2017 update to the 2014 survey has strengthened the institutional and financial capacities of their Centres of Government, whose mandates have progressively shifted from administrative support to policy coordination (OECD, 2018[32]).

Figure 2.2. Key responsibilities delegated to the Centre of Government across OECD Member countries

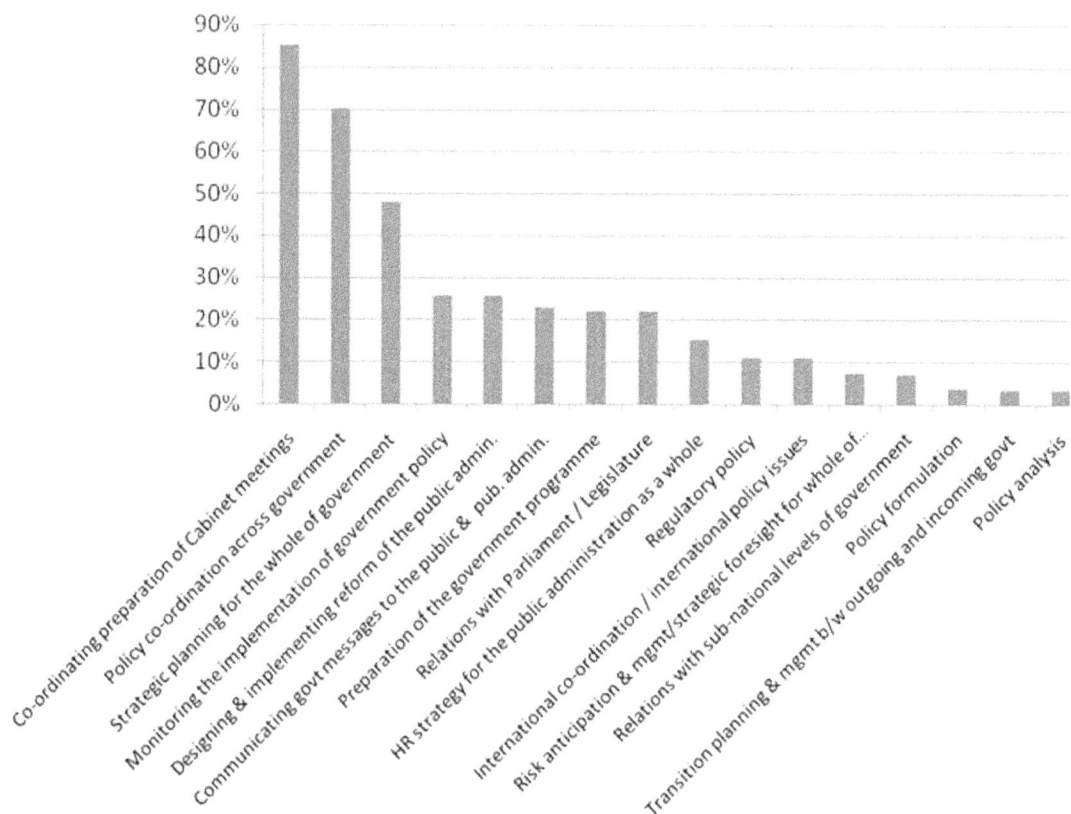

Source: Survey on the Organisation and Functions of the Centre of Government, OECD, 2017 published in OECD (2018[32]), Centre Stage 2: The Organisation and Functions of the Centre of Government in OECD Member countries, OECD Centres of Government

Despite the wide range of institutional CoG structures across OECD Member countries, the 2014 and 2017 OECD surveys on the Centre of Government (OECD, 2014[33] ; OECD, 2018[32]) show several commonalities in their functions and responsibilities for leading whole-of-government co-ordination (Figure 2.2. ). These can be clustered in the following key areas:

- **Driving evidence-based, inclusive and timely decision-making** by the Head of Government;
  - o In most countries, the chief executive is supported by a private office that structures daily business and provides political intelligence and advisory support on an ad hoc basis. Regular Cabinet meetings remain the principal channel for policy discussion.
  - o Legal conformity, regulatory quality and adequate costing are three important technical functions that support decision-making and can be co-ordinated by the CoG.
- **Policy co-ordination across government,** which increasingly includes leading cross-cutting, multidimensional priority strategies;
  - o One test of the effectiveness of the Centre of Government is its ability to play a mediator role between ministries' disagreements.
  - o The CoG is playing more of a leadership role with respect to strategic priorities, including on sensitive policy issues, designing action plans in cooperation with relevant departments and leading in project management.

- o  Several CoGs provide technical and advisory support to line ministries to help them adjust and meet the extra demands of horizontal projects. The main incentives used by the Centre to promote horizontal work are individual or collective performance targets as well as evaluation.
- **Medium-term strategic planning** for the whole-of-government;
  - o  A majority of OECD Member countries adopt strategic documents with a relatively short time horizon, similar to a single electoral term.
  - o  Three planning models are common in OECD Member countries: (i) a thigh-level cluster located close to and reporting directly the Head of Government; (ii) a system of strategy meetings including multiple departments and co-ordinated by the CoG; (iii) a specific unit dedicated to horizon scanning.
- **Monitoring the implementation of government policy** for impact and results;
  - o  Monitoring can take different forms: regular reports delivered to the CoG, cabinet meetings to discuss on the achievement of particular targets, and more specific performance management mechanisms, which could include planning expenditure, input and outcome indicators.
- **Strategic communications**: the Centre of Government is also playing an increasing role in strategic communications both internally and with the public, including managing the government's social media strategies.
- **Leading transition planning**: CoGs are also more frequently called upon to manage strategic support to incoming governments following general elections in order to ensure a smooth transition and transfer of power between governments, thereby sustaining stability across the electoral cycle.

---

### Box 2.6. Policy Coherence for Sustainable Development

Target 17.14 of the SDGs calls on states to enhance policy coherence for sustainable development as a means of implementation This require collaboration and co-ordination across policy sectors and different levels of government. Moreover, policy coherence implies balancing short-term objectives with long-term sustainability objectives in a way that accounts for the impact of domestic policies on global well-being. The 2019 amended *OECD Recommendation of the Council on Policy Coherence for Sustainable Development* highlights the importance of:

- Develop a strategic vision for achieving the SDGs in an integrated and coherent manner
- Develop effective and inclusive institutional mechanisms to address policy interactions across sectors and align actions between levels of government
- Develop a set of responsive and adaptive tools to anticipate asses and address domestic, transboundary and long-term impacts of policies

Source: OECD (2019[79]), Policy Coherence for Sustainable Development 2019: Empowering People and Ensuring Inclusiveness and Equality, OECD Publishing, Paris, https://doi.org/10.1787/a90f851f-en ; OECD, 2019[3], OECD Recommendation of the Council on Policy Coherence for Sustainable Development, https://www.oecd.org/gov/pcsd/oecd-recommendation-on-policy-coherence-for-sustainable-development.htm.

## Core questions for consideration

- Has your government developed civil-service capacities within the public administration to organise and lead high-level strategic policy discussion and planning?
- Are there mechanisms at your government for the coordination of cross-governmental policy initiatives, such as policy co-ordination groups or committees?
- Does your government generate incentives to promote co-ordination across ministries and agencies, such as financial, or individual or collective performance targets?
- Has your government established clear mechanisms such as clear work plans for the implementation of the government programme, performance targets or monitoring instruments to ensure that the government's policy priorities are implemented?

## Innovation and change management

Public-sector innovation is about introducing and implementing new ideas whose impact help promote and improve sound public governance by reinforcing the strategic agility and forward-looking nature of the state. It is about how to introduce, and how to respond to, discontinuous change while promoting citizen-centred approaches in the design and implementation of public services.

- This change can range from the more incremental (significantly altering or introducing an entirely new process), to the radical (a whole new way of understanding the world).
- The change can be about disruption (i.e. new technology and associated operating models), about transformation (e.g. moving from analogue processes to digital interactions), or about defining and pursuing strategic priorities and ambitions when there were none before.

Evidence suggests that promoting public-sector innovation is a key priority in promoting sound public governance in many OECD Member countries. While market forces, notably competition, shape private-sector performance, the public sector needs to implement a range of mechanisms that supports, or at least establishes the conditions for, dynamic and disruptive capacity to change in ways that improve the government's performance in serving citizens and businesses successfully in a fast-changing world. Governments now have to grapple with a number of drivers that requires a more structured and consistent approach to managing change and encouraging innovation:

- *Changing functions* – in an environment of change, governments must also change how they operate;
- *Running to stay in place* – in an evolving economy, governments have to change policy settings just in order to maintain results;
- *No room for spectators* – in order to remain effective decision-makers, governments have to have actual knowledge of innovation; they cannot wait for the answers to be given to them;
- *People expect more* – many politicians, citizens and public servants want and expect things to change;
- *Risk of a mismatch* – a government that does not innovate is one that is at risk of always being behind, always reacting yet forever disappointing;
- *Innovation as a core competency* – the need for innovation can strike anywhere, therefore everyone must be ready to play a part.

Much is still being learned about how best to create the conditions for innovation, and the skills, capabilities, tools and resources needed to undertake it successfully. Experience from across OECD Member countries indicates that innovation takes place across all levels of government. There is a role for the central government to create the conditions for it to emerge (Box 2.7). Research has found that the main innovation enablers in government are linked to factors related to how people are managed, whether internal regulations work, the role of budgets in creating space for innovation, how project management practices can be designed to deal with risks, and how to create safe spaces to experiment (innovation labs and units).

However considering these factors in isolation only provides a partial view of where innovation is most required or wanted, and may result in shifting blockages from one part of the system to another. The *OECD Declaration on Public Sector Innovation* (2019[40]) [OECD/LEGAL/0450] seeks to help governments and public organisations improve innovation to address a variety of challenges and leverage opportunities. The declaration establishes five principles and associated actions which can inform innovation and its management:

- Embrace and enhance innovation within the public sector
- Encourage and equip all public sector servants to innovate
- Cultivate new partnerships and involve different voices
- Support exploration, iteration and testing
- Diffuse lessons and share practices

In addition, a systems perspective can bolster the capacity and ability of the civil service to identify, develop and apply new approaches as needed, both to meet current mandates and respond to new threats and opportunities[4]. The OECD has identified four areas that administrations should concentrate on if innovation is to be a consistent and reliable resource for governments:

- *Clarity* – is there a clear signal being sent to actors in the public service about innovation and how it fits with other priorities?
- *Parity* – does innovation have equal footing with other considerations for proposed courses of action?
- *Suitability* – are the capabilities, systems, and infrastructure suitable for the options that are available?
- *Normality* – is innovation seen as integral rather than as an occasionally accepted deviation from the norm?

Moreover, in 2017, the OECD Observatory of Public Sector Innovation published a beta model of skills to promote and enable innovation in public sector organisations (OECD, 2017[41]). The OECD beta skills model for public sector innovation is based around six "core" skill areas which enable civil servants to support increased levels of innovation in the public sector:

- Iteration: Incrementally and experimentally developing policies, products and services
- Data literacy: ensuring decisions are data-driven and that data isn't an after thought
- User centricity: Public services should be focused on solving and servicing user needs
- Curiosity: seeking out and trying new ideas or ways of working
- Storytelling : explaining change in a way that builds support
- Insurgency: challenging the status quo and working with unusual partners

> ## Box 2.7. Innovation in the public sector in Canada
>
> **Impact Canada**
>
> Announced in Budget 2017, Impact Canada is a whole-of-government effort that helps departments to accelerate the adoption of innovative approaches to deliver meaningful results to Canadians. The initiative reflects the need for and value of innovation in achieving government priorities and improving societal outcomes for citizens. Impact Canada promotes a wide range of innovative approaches including:
>
> - Challenge prizes which reward the first or best solution to a specific problem based on a set of pre-determined criteria;
> - Pay-for-Results Instruments, which are approaches to funding that shift the focus towards issue payments based on the achievements of positive and measurable results;
> - Behavioural insights, which is the application of findings from psychology, economics, and other social sciences to the work of government.
>
> **Canada's Deputy Ministers Task Force on Public Sector Innovation (TF-PSI)**
>
> In November 2017, Canada launched the Deputy Ministers Task Force on public Sector Innovation (TF-PSI). The Task Force aims to play an action-oriented role in experimenting with innovative approaches, and helping the government achieve its policy priorities. The Task Force supports relevant departments along two major themes :
>
> - (1) Core systems transformation and
> - (2) Disruptive policy solutions
>
> Source: Example of country practice provided by the Government of Canada as part of the Policy Framework's consultation process

Innovation and change management are two important but distinct enablers for effective reform. Change management is generally about transitioning to a known desired state or outcome, whereas innovation is an exploratory process of learning in a complex and uncertain context. Both play an essential role in effective government, though both require differing types of support and preconditions to be undertaken successfully.

Changes and reforms can at times be unpopular, or take time to produce results. A key challenge for governments in managing change successfully is to sustain legitimacy while enhancing support for reforms despite political and policy roadblocks or bottlenecks. Effective change management aims to keep the momentum for reform going, while overcoming opposition to change, whether internal or from the public. In the public sector, this is especially difficult as simultaneous change processes often occur at once. The OECD report "Making Reform Happen" (2010[83]) suggests that success in change management often depends on the existence of an electoral mandate, effective communication, sound institutions and leadership, prioritisation and sequencing of reforms, and how effectively reform agents interact with opponents to the reforms being pursued.

While change management is a long-standing focus and activity within the public sector, governments across the OECD are increasingly examining how to take a more sophisticated and institutional approach to change-management issues and strategies. Governments have begun to move away from top-down change-management processes to encompass a broader view of change which involves integrating bottom-up and top-down activities, including systematic problem identification, ideas generation, filtering of alternative solutions and their implementation.

Future iterations of the Policy Framework will present country practice in change management as an important, if still emerging, area of public governance and in so doing will present evidence of success where it exists in managing change and of the impact of successful change-management approaches on improving outcomes for citizens.

## Core questions for consideration

- Does the public sector have the capacity to absorb new trends, address underlying shifts, and track potential changes in citizen expectations and needs?
- How does your government learn from emerging practices, and mainstream the lessons into core practices?
- Does your government support (advising, guiding, and resourcing) agencies, public servants, and actors at the local level to enable them to test and apply new ways of doing things in order to deliver public value?

## Additional resources

OECD Legal Instruments:

- OECD Recommendation of the Council on Policy Coherence for Sustainable Development (2019) [OECD/LEGAL/0381]
- OECD Recommendation of the Council on Effective Public Investment across Levels of Government (2014) [OECD/LEGAL/0402]
- OECD Recommendation of the Council on Public Integrity (2017) [OECD/LEGAL/0435]
- OECD Recommendation of the Council on Open Government (2017) [OECD/LEGAL/0438]
- OECD Recommendation of the Council on Digital Government Strategies (2014) [OECD/LEGAL/0406]
- OECD Recommendation of the Council on Principles for Transparency and Integrity in Lobbying (2010) [OECD/LEGAL/0379]
- OECD Declaration on Public Sector Innovation (2019) [OECD/LEGAL/0450]
- OECD Recommendation of the Council on Public Service Leadership and Capability (2019) [OECD/LEGAL/0445]
- OECD Recommendation of the Council on Public Integrity (2017) [OECD/LEGAL/0435]
- OECD Recommendation of the Council on Gender Equality in Public Life (2015) [OECD/LEGAL/0410]
- OECD Recommendation of the Council on Digital Government Strategies (2014) [OECD/LEGAL/0406]
- OECD Recommendation of the Council on Regulatory Policy and Governance (2012) [OECD/LEGAL/0390]

Other relevant OECD tools:

- The OECD Observatory of Public Sector Innovation (OPSI)
- OECD Embracing Innovation in Government: Global Trends (2019)
- OECD Core Skills for Public Sector Innovation (2017)

- OECD Fostering innovation in the public sector (2017)
- Managing Change in OECD Governments. An Introductory Framework (2008)
- "Modernising Government", in Making Reform Happen, Lessons from OECD Countries (2010)
- SIGMA The Principles of Public Administration, OECD Publishing, Paris (2017)
- SIGMA Methodological Framework for the Principles of Public Administration, OECD Publishing, Paris (2019)
- OECD Policy Advisory Systems: Supporting Good Governance and Sound Public Decision Making, OECD Public Governance Reviews (2017).
- OECD Preventing Policy Capture, Integrity in Public Decision Making (2017).
- Summary of OECD conference on Evidence-Informed Policy Making (2017)
- OECD Core Skills for Public Sector Innovation (2017)
- OECD Centre Stage, Driving Better Policies from the Centre of Government (2014)
- SIGMA The Principles of Public Administration, OECD Publishing, Paris, (2017)

## References

Alessandro, M., M. Lafuente and C. Santiso (2013), The Role of the Center of Government A Literature Review, Institutions for Development , Washington, DC, http://www.iadb.org (accessed on 4 October 2019). [34]

Beuselinck, E. (2008), Shifting public sector coordination and the underlying drivers of change: a neo-institutional perspective, Katholieke Universiteit Leuven. [37]

OECD (2019), Effective Public Investment Across Levels of Government : Implementing the OECD Principles, Centre for Entrepreneurships, SMES, Regions and Cities, https://www.oecd.org/effective-public-investment-toolkit/ (accessed on 4 October 2019). [39]

OECD (2019), Policy Coherence for Sustainable Development 2019: Empowering People and Ensuring Inclusiveness and Equality, OECD Publishing, Paris, https://dx.doi.org/10.1787/a90f851f-en. [79]

OECD (2019), Recommendation of the Council on Public Service Leadership and Capability. [9]

OECD (2019), Declaration on Public Sector Innovation, https://legalinstruments.oecd.org/en/instruments/OECD-LEGAL-0450 (accessed on 4 October 2019). [40]

OECD (2019), Recommendation of the Council on Policy Coherence for Sustainable Development, https://www.oecd.org/gov/pcsd/oecd-recommendation-on-policy-coherence-for-sustainable-development.htm. [3]

OECD (2018), Centre Stage 2, OECD Centres of Government. [32]

OECD (2017), Multi-level Governance Reforms: Overview of OECD Country Experiences, OECD Multi-level Governance Studies, OECD Publishing, Paris, https://doi.org/10.1787/9789264272866-en. [38]

OECD (2017), Preventing Policy Capture: Integrity in Public Decision Making, OECD Public Governance Reviews, OECD Publishing, Paris, https://dx.doi.org/10.1787/9789264065239- [36]

en.

OECD (2017*), Systems Approaches to Public Sector Challenges: Working with Change*, OECD    [2]
Publishing, Paris, https://dx.doi.org/10.1787/9789264279865-en.

OECD (2017), *Core Skills for Public Sector Innovation*, Observatory of Public Sector Innovation,    [41]
OECD Publishing, Paris.

OECD (2017), Government at a Glance 2017, OECD Publishing, Paris,    [1]
https://dx.doi.org/10.1787/gov_glance-2017-en.

OECD (2017), Recommendation of the Council on Public Integrity.    [11]

OECD (2016), Open Government:The global context and the way forward.    [23]

OECD (2015), Recommendation of the Council on Gender Equality in Public Life.    [25]

OECD (2014), Centre Stage: Driving Better Policies from the Centre of Governemnt.    [33]

OECD (2014), Recommendation of the Council on Digital Government Strategies.    [31]

OECD (2014), Vision, Leadership, Innovation: Driving Public Sector Performance.    [30]

OECD (2012), Recommendation of the Council on Regulatory Policy and Governance.    [27]

OECD (2011), Estonia: Towards a Single Government Approach, OECD Public Governance    [78]
Reviews, OECD Publishing, Paris, https://dx.doi.org/10.1787/9789264104860-en.

OECD (2010), Making Reform Happen: Lessons from OECD Countries, OECD Publishing,    [83]
Paris, https://dx.doi.org/10.1787/9789264086296-en.

Parkhurst, J. (2017), The politics of evidence: from evidence-based policy to the good    [35]
governance of evidence, Abingdon: Routledge,
http://eprints.lse.ac.uk/68604/1/Parkhurst_The_Politics_of_Evidence.pdf (accessed on
4 October 2019).

## Notes

---

[1] *OECD Recommendation of the Council on Public Integrity* (2017[11])

[2] The elements of such an enabling environment are outlined in the *OECD Recommendation on Gender Equality in Public Life* and its accompanying Toolkit

[3] http://www.oecd.org/gov/pem/performanceandleadership.htm.

[4] A systems approach "analyses the different elements of the system underlying a policy problem, as well as the dynamics and interactions of these elements that produce a particular outcome. The term "systems approaches" denotes a set of processes, methods and practices that aim to affect systems change" (OECD, 2017[2]).

62

# Part II Sound Public Governance for Policy Formulation, Implementation and Evaluation

# 3 Toward sound problem identification, policy formulation and design

This chapter identifies different management tools and policy instruments adopted by OECD Members to enhance the quality of problem identification, policy formulation and design. Practices presented in this chapter show that the following management tools can improve the quality of policy formulation and design: strategic planning, skills for developing policy, and digital capacities. This chapter also lays out how regulatory policy and budgetary governance can be used strategically to eschew governance failures during the policy formulation process. Regulatory policy and governance can help to ensure that regulations meet the desired objectives and new challenges as efficiently as possible and budgetary governance is an instrument to translate political commitment, goals and objectives into decisions on what policies receive financing and how these resources are generated.

**The first step in sound policy-making is properly identifying a problem and designing the right response(s) to address it.** Multiple factors influence the identification of policy challenges and their incorporation into the public agenda, including:

- The capacity of representative institutions (for instance political parties, trade unions or trade associations) to articulate the challenge;
- The media's role in translating and communicating the challenge in a way that resonates with citizens;
- The availability of data and evidence to enable the government to confirm that the issue is real and that it is in the government's purview to address it;
- Effective stakeholder-engagement that enables the government to launch and sustain dialogue with relevant civil-society actors and with citizens on the issue and on how to address it successfully; and
- The capacity of the government to anticipate challenges through, for example, strategic foresight, horizon scanning and debates on alternative futures, including with civil society.

Chapters 1 and 2 of this Framework have highlighted governance practices that support open, equitable and evidence-informed problem identification as a way, inter alia, to avoid the capture of public policies by interest groups. Section 3.1.2 of this chapter also focuses on the importance of civil servants having the right analytical skills to define policy problems, notably to detect and understand their root causes.

Once an issue has been correctly identified, defined and framed, governments can determine adequate courses of action to solve the problem and/or implement a reform. . The policy formulation stage is the process by which governments translate long, medium and short-term policy goals into concrete courses of action.

The government is not a monolithic decision-maker, as such, the **policy formulation** process provides an opportunity for governments to collaborate with citizens, business and civil society organisations (CSOs), to innovate and deliver improved public service outcomes. Examples of co-production and co-decision-making range from referenda to consultation processes in which the course of action is developed and deliberated with a wide range of stakeholders and representative groups (OECD, 2011[44]). As explained in Chapter 2, engaging stakeholders can also constitutes a means to avoid policy capture during the policy-making process. This process can produce draft legislations, regulations, resource allocations or roadmaps and frameworks for future negotiations on more detailed plans. In an ideal setting, policy formulation therefore includes the identification, assessment, discussion and drafting of policy options to address societal needs and challenges.

One essential part of the formulation stage is the **policy design**, which deals with planning the implementation/enforcement, monitoring and evaluation stages. Ideally, based on a broad range of political and technical input, the government – and in particular, elected officials and senior management within it – will decide which tools and instruments they intend to use, and what financial and human resources they should allocate to implement and enforce a policy. Translating these visions and plans into achievable policies constitutes one of the greatest challenges in policy-making. Likewise, governments should consider evaluation mechanisms for new regulations and policies at the policy-formulation and design stage. Where relevant, specific regulations, such as sun-setting clauses should also be incorporated in the design of a policy. Decision makers usually have to choose among a wide array of options provided by an increasing range of policy advisors, from civil servants to such external actors as lobbying firms, private sector representatives, advisory or expert groups, NGOs, think tanks, academia, or political parties among others stakeholders. For instance, evidence shows that advisory bodies operating at arms' length from government are increasingly playing a role in policy-making and can constitute enablers for inclusive and sound policy-making (OECD, 2017[45]). The enablers outlined in Chapter 2 of this Framework emphasise the role that Centre of Government and institutional leadership play in driving the definition of strategic priorities and in leading the pursuit of medium term strategic planning to implement them.

Analysing and weighing the political, economic, social and environmental benefits and costs of different policy actions thus forms the core of the policy formulation phase. OECD evidence suggests that without a proper governance framework, public decisions and regulations are especially prone to be influenced or captured by special interests (CleanGovBiz, 2012[46]). Moreover, governance capacity failures such as limited financial, human and technological resources, or governance design failures such as the shortcomings of the institutional framework or inadequate regulations are a few of the numerous barriers to policy design that consequently hamper efficient policy implementation and service delivery

Having identified some of these barriers over the past decades, the OECD has pursued specific work in the governance of (1) management tools and (2) policy instruments that can enhance the quality of policy formulation and design:

- Sections 3.1.1, 3.1.2 and 3.1.3 of this chapter focus on ways to bolster strategic planning, civil servants skills and digital capacities to improve policy formulation and design.
- Section 3.2.1 lays out the way in which regulatory policy can be a strategic policy instrument to eschew governance design failures during the policy formulation process.
- Section 3.2.2 of this chapter addresses the way in which budgetary governance can be used as a policy instrument to mitigate governance capacity shortcomings.

To ensure the effectiveness of, and support for, the course of action chosen by decision-makers, it is important that stakeholders perceive the policy action as valid, efficient and implementable. Thus, the policy formulation and design stage represents an opportunity for policymakers to ensure that practices associated with public governance values (chapter 1) are adopted, mainstreamed and integrated into the implementation process. In addition to the practices that will be highlighted in this chapter, successful practices and aspirations regarding mainstreaming of governance values are codified in the *OECD Recommendation of the Council on Digital Government Strategies* (2014) [OECD/LEGAL/0406], the amended *OECD Recommendation on Promoting Good Institutional Practices for Policy Coherence for Development* (2019) [OECD/LEGAL/0381] – which is under the responsibility of the Development Assistance Committee and in relation to which a revised Recommendation was developed in the Development Assistance Committee and Public Governance Committee - as well as the *Recommendation on Public Integrity* (2017) [OECD/LEGAL/0435], the *Recommendation on Open Government* (2017) [OECD/LEGAL/0438], and the *Recommendation on Gender Equality in the Public Life* (2015) [OECD/LEGAL/0418].

## Management tools for policy formulation and design

In the policy formulation and design stage, management tools constitute means to enhance public sector skills and capacity for policy design. They can serve as direct channels for policy implementation such as is the case of digital learning platforms. Some of the key management tools to improve the quality of policy design and therefore, shape policy outcomes are (1) **strategic planning**, (2) **skills for developing policy**, (3) **digital capacities**.

### Strategic planning

A well-embedded planning practice can be instrumental in translating political commitments and ambitions into both long/medium-term strategies and operational action plans to guide the work of government. As such, strategic planning is a key management tool associated with enablers in sections 2.1 and 2.3 of this Framework. Strategic planning can be relevant to adjust domestic policies to match the multidisciplinary and complex nature of the 2030 agenda. When incorporating the Sustainable Development Goals to domestic plans, governments need to contend with their national realities and constraints as wells existing international commitments (OECD, 2019[47]). In this respect, lessons learned in country practice shows that:

- Prioritisation should be an important part of the early stages of policy formulation, based on the problem-identification. Governments usually do not have resources to address all problems (simultaneously, at least). Prioritisation can lead to more realistic commitments and better-designed interventions which can help governments to develop more credible plans.

- Planning needs to be systematic, ensuring alignment between various plans as well as between long-, medium- and short-term policy priorities towards a common goal

- Strategic planning needs to ensure that policy instruments such as budgeting, regulations and workforce planning are oriented towards this strategy. Principle 2 of the *OECD Recommendation on Budgetary Governance* (2015[48]) [OECD/LEGAL/0410] aims to help policymakers use budget as a substantial policy instrument to achieve medium-term strategic priorities of the government, including those reflecting the SDGs.

- Supreme Auditing Institutions can also play a critical role in designing a more strategic decision-making environment. Through their audit activities, these institutions are able to evaluate the adequacy of processes for long-term vision setting and for planning to transition goals into actions (OECD, 2016[18]).

- Recent experiences in OECD Member countries show that when the planning process is open and includes stakeholder engagement, such as citizen-driven approaches through citizen participation mechanisms, strategic planning can enhance the legitimacy of policy-making and increase the sustainability of policies beyond the electoral cycle (OECD, 2016[23]).

---

### Box 3.1. Norway's Instructions for Official Studies

On 19 February 2016, Norway adopted the Instructions for the Preparation of Central Government Measures ("Instructions for Official Studies"). The Instructions govern a broad range of central government measures and regulate, among other things, the timing of the policy development process, stakeholder coordination, impact analyses, public hearings and proposals for alternatives. The Instructions and associated guidelines aim to promote sound decision-making requirements for central government measures. This implies that the rationale for decisions is established prior to deciding which measure should be implemented.

Source: Example of country practice provided by the Government of Norway as part of the Policy Framework's consultation process

---

### *Skills for developing policy*

Civil servants address problems of unprecedented complexity in increasingly pluralistic societies. In parallel, governance tools have evolved to be more digital, open and networked. The first challenge is therefore to identify which skills are needed for policy formulation and design, today and into the future. The OECD highlights a set of skills for a high-performing civil service: (1) skills for policy development, (2) skills for citizen engagement and service delivery, (3) skills for commissioning and contracting, and (4) skills for managing networks.

Skills for policy development are particularly important for the policy formulation stage. They combine traditional aptitudes, such as the capacity for providing evidence-based, balanced and objective advice while withstanding political and partisan pressure, with a new set of skills to meet expectations for digital, open and innovative government, technological transformations and the increasing complexity policy challenges The emphasis on evidence-informed decisions and innovation reflect the priorities established in sections 2.2 and 2.4 of this Framework. Policymakers need to know when and how to deploy institutional and administrative tools for policy formulation and design. Hence the importance of developing professional, strategic and innovation skills for:

- **Defining policy problems**: civil servants need to be capable of detecting and understanding the root causes of policy challenges. This requires "analytical skills that can synthesise multiple disciplines and/or perspectives into a single narrative" (OECD, 2017[49]) including the capacity to interpret and integrate different and sometimes conflicting visions correctly, and to refocus and reframe policies. This also includes networking and digital skills to identify the right stakeholders and the right experts outside the civil service for engagement in policy formulation.

- **Designing Solutions**: civil servants need the skills to understand potential future scenarios, and find resilient solutions to future challenges. These might include foresight skills and systems and design thinking to understand and influence the interactions among internal and external stakeholders and reconcile different sector expertise. They need to be able to identify and harness internal and external resources to facilitate the refining and implementation of the solution. They need to understand what has worked in the recent past and identify best practice that can be adapted to current problems.

- **Influencing the policy agenda**: Senior civil servants and those working on policy development need the skills to understand the political environment and identify the right opportunities to move forward with policy initiatives and to advise politicians on options and trade-offs. Beyond the analysis of technocratic issues, civil servants therefore need to be able to take into consideration political and social values issues. This requires judgement skills to provide timely advice, recognise and manage risk and uncertainty, and design policy proposals in a way that responds to the political imperatives of the moment. Moreover, skills for communicating policy ideas, such as visual presentations and storytelling, can be central for the interaction with elected and politically-appointed decision-makers.

Once governments have identified the skills needed for policy formulation and design, the second challenge is to establish how governments can best invest in these skills to improve outcomes (see Box 3.2 for an example). The OECD *Recommendation on Public Service Leadership and Capability* (2019[9]) [OECD/LEGAL/0445] provides guidance to Adherents on how to invest in public service capability to develop an effective and trusted public service. This includes specific principles and guidance to:

- Continuously identify skills and competencies needed to transform political vision into services which deliver value to society;

- Attract and retain employees with the required skills and competencies;

- Recruit, select and promote trough transparent, open and merit-based processes, to guarantee fair and equal treatment;

- Develop the necessary skills and competencies by creating a learning culture and environment in the public service;

- Assess, reward and recognise performance, talent and initiative.

Box 3.2. Framework for Client-Friendly Public Administration 2030 in the Czech Republic

The Framework for Client-Friendly Public Administration 2030 is a strategic document defining development of Czech public administration in the period 2021-2030. It highlights a number of measures to bolster skills for developing policy:

- Implementation of evidence-informed decision-making in public administration - including specialised training of public officials responsible for analytical research and reports (strategic goal (SG) 3.1.1)

- Establishment of Working group on cooperation of analytical units and establishment of analytical teams within the civil service - collaborative network and web platform for sharing the analytical data (SG 3.1.3, 3.1.4)

- Development of skills to provide timely policy advice and analysis (SG 3.1.1)

- In order to develop effective and trusted public service – implementation of training for front desk public officials with the aim of improvement of client-oriented communication and services; new tool for centralised civil servants´ training targeting common cross-sectional issues using e-learning (SG 1.1.5, 4.3.1)

Source: Example of country practice provided by the Government of the Czech Republic as part of the Policy Framework's consultation process

## Digital capacities

In order to allow relevant stakeholders to collaborate actively with policymakers in the formulation of public policies, the government's digital capacities are fundamental. The *OECD Recommendation on Open Government* (2017[22]) [OECD/LEGAL/0438] emphasises that new technologies and digital progress allow for a more participative and collaborative policy design process through more meaningful stakeholder engagement. Indeed, digital tools generate better access to information and therefore increase citizen participation in the formulation of public policies. This can contribute to obtain equitable decision-making, which is one of the enablers of sound policy-making in Section 2.2. of this Framework).

Box 3.3. Digitalisation and E-Cases in Latvian courts

The digitalisation process of the court system in Latvia is exemplified by the launching of the court e-services portal manas.tiesas.lv, which is free of charge and allows the general public to track any court proceedings in any court of Latvia. This initiative aims to provide direct access to the courts through the use of technologies and improve information and service delivery to citizens and businesses.

Additionally, since 2018, Latvia has been in the process of creating a unified electronic proceedings system for the courts. It aims to reduce the length of proceedings and provide wider access to information. This initiative will include electronic data exchange between relevant institutions, access to case materials and electronic updates for participants, as well as statistical data in open data format.

Source: Example of country practice provided by the Government of Latvia as part of the Policy Framework's consultation process; Tiesu Administracija; The court Administration Judicial System in Latvia https://www.ta.gov.lv/UserFiles/TA_buklets_ENG.pdf

The new digital environment enables and empowers rapidly evolving dynamics and relations between stakeholders to which the public sector has to rapidly adapt (OECD, 2014[31]). The *OECD Recommendation on Digital Government Strategie*s (2014[31]) [OECD/LEGAL/0406] stresses that new digital capacities also change expectations on government's ability to deliver public value. As a result, governments are encouraged to integrate efficiency to other societal policy objectives in the governing of digital technologies. A sound digital government strategy therefore goes hand in hand with the enablers change management and innovation that are discussed in Section 2.4 of this Framework.

---

### Box 3.4. Norway's web portal for public accounts

The Norwegian Government Agency for Financial Management launched the web-portal "statsregnskapet.no" (state public accounts) in October 2017. The portal provides up to date financial data for all ministries and central government agencies, searchable by budget chapter and standard chart of accounts. This resource provides a basis for cross-agency comparison and the analysis of resource consumption trends over time in an open data format.

Source: Example of country practice provided by the Government of Norway as part of the Policy Framework's consultation process.

---

However, often governments are not yet adequately equipped to make use of digital innovations and new technologies. Moreover, as described in Section 3.1.2 of the Framework, civil servants are often insufficiently trained to make use of new technologies. Digital progress and its impact on enhancing the capacity to guide or steer the policy process require governments to assess on a regular basis their digital capacities so that these can be adjusted to reflect the vagaries of a constantly changing digital environment. To this end, governments can secure political commitment to the digital government agenda, by promoting cross-ministerial collaboration and facilitating the co-ordination of relevant levels of government. Failures of government to make the transitions could incur serious security breaches and subsequent loss of citizen trust in public institutions. Digital Government Strategies should therefore reflect a risk management approach which addresses security and privacy concerns (OECD, 2014[31]).

The OECD *Recommendation on Digital Government Strategies* (2014[31]) [OECD/LEGAL/0406] helps governments adopt more coherent and strategic approaches for "digital technologies use in all areas and at all levels of the administration" that stimulate more open, participatory and innovative administrations and that are aligned with governments' own digital capacities. Digital tools alone do not guarantee success, developing strategies and standards for their use is therefore paramount. In order to develop and implement digital government strategies, the *Recommendation on Digital Government Strategies* suggests that governments:

- Ensure greater transparency, openness and inclusiveness of government processes and operations (Principle 1);
- Encourage engagement and participation of public, private and civil society stakeholders in policy-making and public services design and delivery (Principle 2).

### Core questions for consideration

- Does your government have in place a robust multi-year strategic planning framework? Does this framework link strategic plans together and with the national budget?

- Has your government undertaken specific measures to build civil service skills for policy formulation and design (e.g. through recruitment, promotion and training frameworks)?
- Has your government established a legal or policy framework to facilitate the use of ICT as a mean to foster engagement and more participatory approaches in decision-making and the service design and delivery process?
- Does your government evaluate the efficiency of its public procurement system?

## The strategic use of policy instruments

During the problem-identification and policy-formulation phase policymakers not only have to decide what to do in setting the objectives they aim to achieve, they need to consider how best to address the problem by deliberating about costs and effects of proposed solutions. As part of this process, policymakers have to decide which substantial policy instruments can best be deployed to address a problem and implement a solution. Substantial policy instruments or tools are "the actual means or devices that governments make use of in implementing policies" (Howlett, Ramesh and Perl, 2009[42]). In the area of public governance, the OECD highlights the importance of **the policy instruments of budgeting and rule-making** to ensure that policies can meet the desired objectives and new challenges in as efficient as possible.

### *Regulatory policy and governance*

A central policy instrument used by governments to intervene in economic matters and steer societal development are regulations. Policymakers can use regulation as an instrument, by imposing binding rules or limiting access to certain benefits and/or advantages directly or indirectly. When they are proportionate, targeted and smart they can improve social, economic and environmental conditions. When regulations are inadequate, consequences can be severe: non-implementable laws, frequent legislative chances, both of which undermine legal certainty and the business environment. To ensure regulations are not excessively burdensome, the OECD calls for governments to identify and revise public policies that unduly restrict competition by adopting more pro-competitive alternatives. The *OECD Recommendation on Competition Assessment* (2009[50]) [OECD/LEGAL/0376], under the responsibility of the OECD's Competition Committee, encourages further governmental efforts to reduce unduly restrictive regulations and promote beneficial market activity

The 2008 global financial and economic crisis and its underlying failings in governance and regulation have shown the importance of regulatory policy as an instrument for sound policy-making. A "well-functioning national regulatory framework for transparent and efficient markets is central to re-injecting confidence and restoring [economic] growth" (OECD, 2012[27]) Moreover, sound regulations can eventually help policymakers meet fundamental social objectives in areas such as health, social welfare or public safety and represent an important instrument to master environmental challenges.

However, adopting the right regulations as an instrument to solve policy problems is a continuously demanding task. Policymakers have to evaluate if regulation is necessary and to what extent means other than regulatory instruments, such as awareness and communication campaigns, self-regulation or co-regulation, could be more effective and efficient to achieve policy objectives. To help governments implement and advance regulatory practice that meets stated public policy objectives, the *Recommendation on Regulatory Policy and Governance* (OECD, 2012[27]) [OECD/LEGAL/0390]:

- Provides governments with clear and timely guidance on the principles, mechanisms and institutions required to improve the design, enforcement and review of their regulatory framework to the highest standards;
- Advises governments on the effective use of regulation to achieve better social, environmental and economic outcomes; and

- Calls for a "whole-of-government" approach to regulatory reform, with an emphasis on the importance of consultation, co-ordination, communication and co-operation to address the challenges posed by the inter-connectedness of sectors and economies.

Being the first comprehensive international statement on regulatory policy since the financial crisis, the *Recommendation on Regulatory Policy and Governance* advises policymakers on regulation design and quality during the policy formulation phase. The *Recommendation* highlights the importance of the public-governance values highlighted in Chapter 1 and in the *OECD Recommendation on Open Government* (2017[22]) [OECD/LEGAL/0438], including transparency and participation in the regulatory process "to ensure that regulation serves the public interest and is informed by the legitimate to needs of those interested in and affected by regulation".

**Transparency** can positively add to the accountability of policymakers and increase citizens' trust in the regulatory framework. The *Recommendation on Open Government* stresses the role of public consultations to engage stakeholders in all aspects of the policy-making process, including consideration and discussion about alternative options and the drafting process of regulatory proposals. Consultation and engagement eventually improve the transparency and quality of regulations through the collection of ideas, information and evidence from stakeholders regarding public policy-making. In turn, governments should be transparent about the way in which consultations influenced the process to support a lasting dialogue between external stakeholders and public authorities.

**External consultation** is a crucial element to prevent regulators from being subjected to one-sided influences, especially during the formulation phase and therefore to ensure that regulators act in the public interest and serve social cohesion. The *OECD Recommendation on Public Integrity* (2017[11]) [OECD/LEGAL/0435] further highlights the importance of levelling the playing field by granting all stakeholders – in particular, stakeholders with diverging interests – access in the development of public policies. This requires measures to ensure constructive stakeholder engagement in policy-making procedures, as well as instilling integrity and transparency in lobbying activities and political financing. Overall, transparency and stakeholder engagement (also important components of the *OECD Recommendation on Open Government* (2017) [OECD/LEGAL/0438], which is discussed in Section 1.2) can further reinforce trust in government, strengthen the inclusiveness of regulations and help to increase compliance with regulations by developing a sense of ownership

The majority of OECD Member countries have adopted stakeholder-engagement practices for the development of regulations. They use various forms of engagement, ranging from public online consultation to informal participation mechanisms. Countries with the highest scores of stakeholder-engagement in developing regulations have for instance adopted frameworks to open consultation processes to all parties interested and to disclose all stakeholder comments as well as government responses (see Figure 3.1).

### Figure 3.1. Stakeholder engagement in developing subordinate regulations, 2018

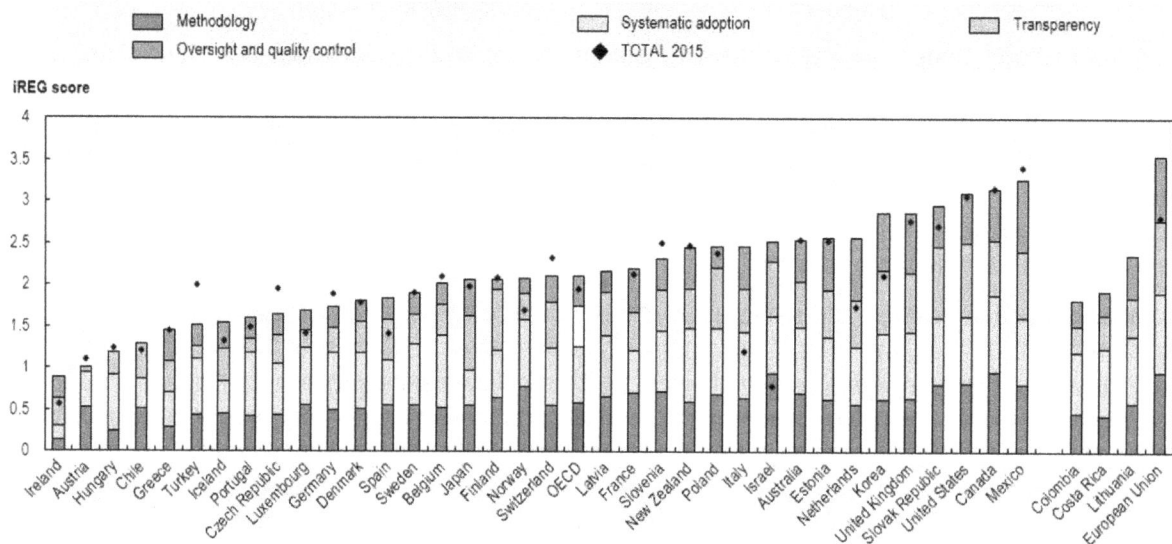

Note: The statistical data for Israel are supplied by and under the responsibility of the relevant Israeli authorities. The use of such data by the OECD is without prejudice to the status of the Golan Heights, East Jerusalem and Israeli settlements in the West Bank under the terms of international law.

Source: (OECD[51]) Indicators of Regulatory Policy and Governance Surveys 2014 and 2017, http://oe.cd/ireg

In order to assess benefits, costs and effect of different regulatory and non-regulatory solutions during the policy formulation stage, ex-ante **Regulatory Impact Assessment (RIA)** offers policymakers a key instrument to promote the best response to specific policy problems. OECD experience has shown that conducting ex-ante RIA improves the governments' capacity to regulate efficiently and enables policymakers to identify the policy solution that is most suitable to reach public policy goals. The OECD Recommendation on Regulatory Policy and Governance (2012[27]) [OECD/LEGAL/0390] suggests governments "integrate Regulatory Impact Assessment (RIA) into the early stages of the policy process for the formulation of new regulatory proposals" and offers guidance for the design and implementation of assessment practices.

RIA can help increase policy coherence by revealing regulatory proposals' trade-offs and identifying potential beneficiaries of regulations. In addition, RIA can also add to a more evidence-informed policy-making and help prevent regulatory failure due to unnecessary regulation, or lack of regulation when regulatory policy would be required. The collection of evidence through the RIA process can enhance the accountability of policy decisions at the formulation phase. Furthermore, external oversight and control bodies such as Supreme Audit Institutions (SAIs) can verify whether a coherent, evidence-based and reliable RIA accompanied the drafting of regulations (OECD, 2017[36]). The OECD Recommendation on Public Integrity (2017[11]) [OECD/LEGAL/0435] emphasises their crucial role in promoting accountable public decision-making.

All OECD Member countries have adopted formal requirements and developed methodologies for conducting RIA (OECD, 2018[52]). Ideally, RIA should not only assess the potential costs and benefits of regulatory proposals, but also try to determine any compliance and enforcement issues associated with a regulation.

### Budgetary Governance

Another policy instrument for sound public governance is budgeting. The budget reflects a government's policy priorities and translates political commitments, goals and objectives into decisions on the financial resources allocated to pursue them, and on how these financial resources are to be generated. It enables the government to establish spending priorities related to the pursuit of its strategic objectives and to proceed with a sequencing of initiatives that takes into account the availability of financial resources as defined in the fiscal framework. As mentioned above in section 3.1.1, governments are more systematically aligning planning priorities with spending priorities by ensuring greater linkages between planning and budgeting. This is particularly the case when governments pursue Performance-Based budgeting (see Box 3.6 on Estonia's efforts in this regard). In conjunction with strategic planning, budgetary governance can improve the extent to which resource allocation promotes the design of policies in support of national Sustainable Development Goals., and ensure the continuity of these policy objectives beyond electoral cycles (OECD, 2019[47]). Fiscal councils, parliamentary budget offices or Supreme Auditing Institutions can fulfil this purpose, by providing oversight to budgetary debates for instance or ensuring the underlying assumptions of the budget are sound. Additionally, effective public internal control and a risk management approach are paramount to ensure states develop efficient policies in a legal, ethical and financially appropriate manner.

---

### Box 3.6. Performance-Based Budgeting in Estonia

Estonia is currently transitioning towards performance-based budgeting. In May 2019, the Government approved Estonia's first performance-based State Budget Strategy 2020-2023 and State Budget for 2020. The transition to an output-based approach requires ministries to reduce the number of programmes' objectives and link these to performance indicators. These reforms aim to achieve more effective and efficient public services, and improve budgetary decision-making.

Source: Example of country practice provided by the Government of Estonia as part of the Policy Framework's consultation process

---

Through budget allocation, policymakers can strategically encourage or discourage particular courses of action. Government spending can, for instance, influence the provision of services or infrastructure in case of market imperfections or failure in areas such as public health or environment protection and serve as leverage to encourage private investment and innovation (Box 3.7). Moreover, public expenditure can positively contribute to spatial, social and economic cohesion. Through the use of fiscal instruments, such as taxes, tariffs, duties and charges, policymakers can also help discourage certain economic or private behaviours.

---

### Box 3.7. OECD Framework for the Governance of Infrastructure

Poor infrastructure governance is one of the most common bottlenecks to achieving long-term development. It affects not only the capacity of the public sector to deliver quality infrastructure but also has a negative impact on investment by the private sector. Good governance promotes value for money and allows financing to flow, poor governance generates waste and discourages investment.

The OECD Framework for the Governance of Infrastructure has been recognised by national governments and other international organisations as the main policy framework to ensure countries invest in the right projects, in a way that is cost effective, affordable and trusted by investors, users and citizens. After 5 years of implementation, it is proposed to update the Framework and, in the process, embody it in an OECD Recommendation. The Framework is designed to help governments improve their management of infrastructure policy from strategic planning all the way to project level delivery. It is built around ten key dimensions across the governance cycle of infrastructure, including determining a long-term national strategic vision for infrastructure; integration of infrastructure policy with other government priorities; co-ordination mechanisms for infrastructure policy within and across levels of government; stakeholder engagement and consultation. It furthermore looks at procedures to monitor performance of the asset throughout its life and measures needed to safeguard integrity at each phase of infrastructure projects; as well as the procedures used to ensure feasibility, affordability and cost efficiency; and under which conditions projects with private participation can lead to better outcomes.

Source: OECD (2017[56]) Getting Infrastructure Right: a Framework for Better Governance.

---

Along with effective expenditure management, tax policy and tax administration reform can be a crucial starting point to improve state capacity and launch needed reforms (OECD, 2013[55]). Moreover, taxation often elicits demands for more responsiveness and accountability coupled with better management of expenditures. Conversely, reliance on taxes creates incentives for governments to be more receptive to demands from the public. However, tax policy must strike a difficult balance between securing revenues without constraining innovation, productivity, and inclusive economic growth. The OECD Centre for Tax Policy and Administration supports the Committee on Fiscal Affairs and its bodies to assist countries in devising sound tax policies and tax administration reforms. For instance, the Global Revenue Statistics Database provides the largest public source of comparable tax revenue data and strengthens governments' capacity to develop and implement tax policy reforms. Additionally, the OECD's Tax Administration Series provides internationally comparative data on aspects of tax systems and their administration in 58 advanced and emerging economies.

A budget oriented towards inclusiveness, can encourage the adoption of more inclusive policies during the policy formulation phase. Adopting a gender perspective with regard to budget decisions, by making use of special processes and analytical tools can help to promote gender-responsive policies that address existing gender inequalities and disparities. The *2018 OECD Budget Practices and Procedures Survey* has shown that nearly half the OECD Member countries (17 countries) had already introduced and adopted gender mainstreaming in the budget process (OECD, 2018[53]).

Figure 3.2. Status of gender budgeting, 2019

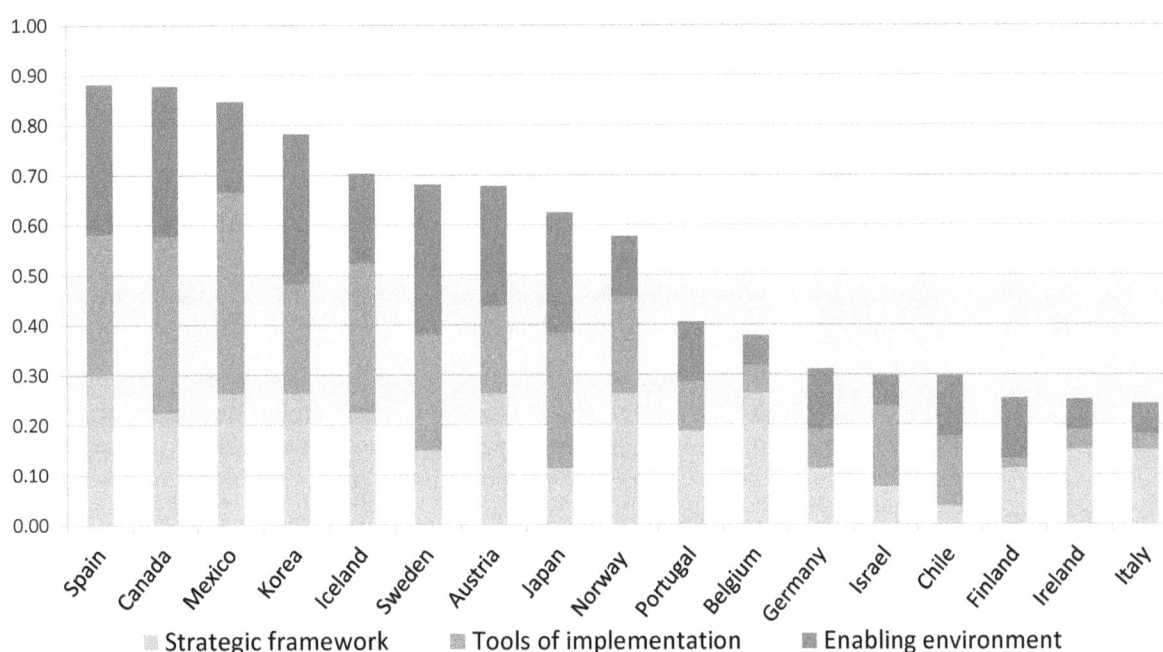

*Note*: Data for the United States are not available; Information on data for Israel: http://dx.doi.org/10.1787/888932315602
*Source*: OECD (2018[53]), OECD Budget Practices and Procedures Survey, Questions 32 and 36, OECD, Paris.

Reflecting **environmental considerations in budget documents** and fiscal frameworks, including the annual budget, can help governments to ensure financing and implementation of policies to attain their environmental objectives. By ensuring that national expenditure and revenue processes are aligned with goals on climate and environmental policies, governments can, moreover, increase the accountability of their commitments and move towards environmentally sustainable development as stipulated by the Paris Agreement on climate change and the UN Sustainable Development Goals. Budgetary governance is crucial to help governments navigate trade-offs between different goals, for instance between industrial growth and biodiversity (OECD, 2019[47]).

Given its central importance for public governance and policy-making, the OECD has developed the *OECD Recommendation on Budgetary Governance* (2015[48]) [OECD/LEGAL/0410], which focuses on "the processes, laws, structures and institutions in place for ensuring that the budgeting system meets its objectives in an effective, sustainable and enduring manner" (OECD, 2015[48]).

**Figure 3.3. The ten principles of good budgetary governance**

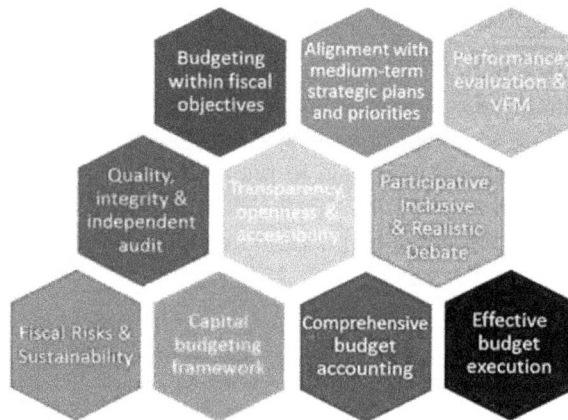

*Source: OECD Recommendation of the Council on Budgetary Governance (OECD, 2015[48])*

Providing a concise overview of good budgetary practices, the *Recommendation on Budgetary Governance* contains ten principles that can serve as guidance for policymakers to make use of the budget system to achieve policy objectives and meet the challenges of the future. In addition to the aforementioned principle 2 (on linking budgeting with national priorities, in line with Section 2.1 of the framework), three principles are of particular importance for the policy formulation phase:

- **Principle 3** calls upon governments to design the capital **budgeting framework in a way that it supports meeting national development needs in a cost-effective and coherent manner**. How governments prioritise, plan, budget, deliver, regulate and evaluate their capital investment is essential to ensure that infrastructure projects meet their timeframe, budget, and service delivery objectives.

- **Principle 4** points to the importance of ensuring that **budget documents and data are open, transparent and accessible, reflecting the value of openness highlighted in Chapter 1 of the framework**. Only with clear, factual budget reports that inform the stage of policy formulation, policymakers can take sufficiently informed budget decision to address policy problems. All budget information should further be presented in comparable format to discuss policy choices with citizens, civil society and other stakeholders to promote effective decision-making and accountability.

- **Principle 5** recommends policy-makers to provide for an **inclusive, participative and realistic debate on budgetary choices** that need to be made in the general public interest. Engagement with parliaments, citizens and civil society organisations in a realistic debate about key priorities, trade-offs, opportunity costs and value for money can increase the quality of budgetary decisions. But public engagement also requires the provision of clarity about relative costs and benefits of the public expenditure programmes and tax expenditures. The provision of citizen-friendly, accessible budget reports is also key to increase citizen interest in budgetary governance.

Box 3.8. Measures to ensure the efficiency of public policies

**Value for Money Unit in Slovakia**

The Value for Money (VfM) unit of the Slovakian Ministry of Finance cooperates with other analytical units across various ministries to identify unnecessary public expenditures of the government. For instance, any investment exceeding 40 million Euros must undergo a cost-benefit analysis carried out by the Value For Money Unit. The Government Office (the CoG unit in the Slovakian Government) has created an Implementation Unit to assess whether or not VfM unit recommendations are carried out.

*Microsimulation of taxes and social contributions in Poland*

Poland's Ministry of Finance has built a microsimulation model to estimate the fiscal costs of policy proposals in the areas of personal income tax and social security contributions. The model is based on individual data from tax returns and the Social Security fund. It is applied to estimate the fiscal costs of changes in personal income tax, social security contributions and health insurance contributions. Advanced modelling tools based on administrative individual data provide a useful assessment of policy interventions and therefore generate evidence-based policy.

Source: Example of country practice provided by the Governments of Slovakia and Poland as part of the Policy Framework's consultation process

## Core questions for consideration

- Has the government established policies, institutions and tools to ensure the quality and coherence of regulatory policy (e.g. the design, oversight and enforcement of rules in all sectors)?
- Has the government established institutions and tools to ensure the involvement of stakeholders in the policy formulation process (with informing affected parties about the policy intentions and embedding an interactive dialogue with stakeholders in the process)?
- To what extent are regulatory impact assessments used to evaluate the wider impacts and consequences of regulations, including on the competition, SMA and investment climate?
- Does your government ensure the alignment of the annual budget, its multi-year budget frameworks as well as its capital-expenditure planning with strategic policy objectives, such as national development plans or the SDGs?
- Has your government established mechanisms to facilitate or promote budget transparency and to discuss the budget with stakeholders such as citizens and civil society organisations during the budget-setting process?
- Has your government implemented - or is planning to implement - specific policies for the development of a gender perspective on budget decisions?
- Has your government implemented – or is planning to implement – specific policies to reflect environmental considerations in the budget documents and fiscal frameworks?

## Additional resources

OECD legal instruments:

- OECD Recommendation of the Council on Public Service Leadership and Capability (2019) [OECD/LEGAL/0445]
- OECD Recommendation of the Council on Open Government (2017) [OECD/LEGAL/0438]
- OECD Recommendation of the Council on Digital Government Strategies (2014) [OECD/LEGAL/0406]
- OECD Recommendation of the Council on Regulatory Policy and Governance (2012) [OECD/LEGAL/0390]
- OECD Recommendation of the Council on Policy Coherence for Development (2019) [OECD/LEGAL/0381]
- OECD Recommendation of the Council on Public Integrity (2017) [OECD/LEGAL/0435]
- OECD Recommendation of the Council on Budgetary Governance (2015) [OECD/LEGAL/0410]
- OECD Recommendation of the Council on Regulatory Policy and Governance (2012) [OECD/LEGAL/0390]
- OECD Recommendation of the Council on Competition Assessment (2009) [OECD/LEGAL/0376]
- OECD Recommendation of the Council on Improving the Quality of Government Regulation (1995) [OECD/LEGAL/0278]

Other relevant OECD tools:

- OECD Public Governance Review: Skills for a High Performing Civil Service (2017)
- OECD Public Procurement Toolbox (2016)
- SIGMA Strategy Toolkit (2018)
- OECD Digital Government Toolkit (2018)
- OECD Best Practice Principles on Stakeholder Engagement in Regulatory Policy (forthcoming)
- OECD Budget Transparency Toolkit (2017)
- OECD CleanGovBiz Toolkit "Regulatory Policy: Improving Governance" (2012)
- OECD Framework for the Governance of Infrastructure (2017)
- OECD Global Revenue Statistics Database
- OECD Open Government: The Global Context and the Way Forward, OECD Publishing (2016)
- OECD Principles for Public Governance of Public-Private Partnerships (2012)
- OECD Regulatory Policy Outlook (2018)
- OECD Toolkit for Mainstreaming and Implementing Gender Equality (2015)
- OECD Tax Administration 2019: Comparative information on OECD and other Advanced and Emerging Economies (2019)
- SIGMA Strategy Toolkit (2018)

# References

CleanGovBiz (2012), Regulatory policy: improving governance, http://www.cleangovbiz.org (accessed on 4 October 2019).    [46]

Howlett, M., M. Ramesh and A. Perl (2009), Studying Public Policy, Oxford University Press.    [42]

OECD (2019), Governance as an SDG Accelerator : Country Experiences and Tools, OECD Publishing, Paris, https://dx.doi.org/10.1787/0666b085-en.    [47]

OECD (2019), Recommendation of the Council on Public Service Leadership and Capability.    [9]

OECD (2018), *OECD Regulatory Policy Outlook 2018*, OECD Publishing, Paris, https://dx.doi.org/10.1787/9789264303072-en.    [52]

OECD (2018), OECD Budget Practices and Procedures Survey, Questions 32 and 36, OECD Publishing, Paris.    [53]

OECD (2017), *Getting Infrastructure Right: A framework for better governance*, OECD Publishing, Paris, https://dx.doi.org/10.1787/9789264272453-en.    [56]

OECD (2017), *Recommendation of the Council on Public Integrity*.    [11]

OECD (2017), Recommendation of the Council on Open Government.    [22]

OECD (2017), Skills for a High Performing Civil Service, OECD Publishing, Paris.    [49]

OECD (2017), Policy Advisory Systems: Supporting Good Governance and Sound Public Decision Making, OECD Public Governance Reviews, OECD Publishing, Paris, https://dx.doi.org/10.1787/9789264283664-en.    [45]

OECD (2016), Open Government:The global context and the way forward, OECD Publishing, Paris.    [23]

OECD (2016), Supreme Audit Institutions and Good Governance: Oversight, Insight and Foresight, OECD Public Governance Reviews, OECD Publishing, Paris, https://dx.doi.org/10.1787/9789264263871-en.    [18]

OECD (2016), *Survey on Gender Budgeting*, OECD.    [57]

OECD (2015), Recommendation of the Council on Budgetary Governance.    [48]

OECD (2014), Recommendation of the Council on Digital Government Strategies.    [31]

OECD (2013), "Taxation and governance", in *Tax and Development: Aid Modalities for Strengthening Tax Systems*, OECD Publishing, Paris, https://dx.doi.org/10.1787/9789264177581-6-en.    [55]

OECD (2012), *Recommendation of the Council on Regulatory Policy and Governance*.    [27]

OECD (2011), Together for Better Public Services: Partnering with Citizens and Civil Society, OECD Public Governance Reviews, OECD Publishing, Paris, https://dx.doi.org/10.1787/9789264118843-en.    [44]

OECD (2009), *Recommendation of the Council on Competition Assessment*.    [50]

OECD *Indicators of Regulatory Policy and Governance*, http://www.oecd.org/gov/regulatory-policy/indicators-regulatory-policy-and-governance.htm (accessed on 7 October 2019). [51]

# 4 Toward sound policy implementation

Even the best-designed policy will fail if the government machinery does not enable the translation of policy decisions into action. Practices presented in this chapter indicate that governments can develop and deploy tools and practices in a strategic and integrated way to enhance the quality and impact of policies and services. The first section of this chapter underscores the role and importance of developing civil service leadership and skills; digital tools; public procurement; public-private partnerships and public-civil partnerships; agile and innovative approaches. It also highlights, as a case study, the importance of having a strategic approach to the implementation of the SDGs. The chapter then underscores monitoring as a means that helps policymakers track progress and make adjustments when necessary during the implementation phase.

If sound public governance is about **doing the right thing** through sound decision-making, it is also about **doing things right** to ensure that policies and services continue to meet people's needs successfully in an increasingly complex and, constantly changing environment that is often fraught with uncertainty. In this regard, people largely evaluate governments by their success or failure to deal with urgencies and problems and their effectiveness in carrying out their policy initiatives.

Successful policy implementation is largely dependent on the government having the right tools at hand to identify the nature and dimensions of those challenges and to formulate and design adequate policy responses to address them. As underscored in Chapter 2 on the Enablers of Sound Public Governance, OECD evidence suggest that such enablers as sustained political commitment, leadership, effective co-ordination and innovation are essential to drive and sustain the implementation process.

However, even the best-designed policy will fail if government machinery does not enable the translation of policy decisions into action. All governance elements explained in the previous chapters, such as the reform enablers, regulation, and effective budgeting, are key for policy implementation. Moreover, OECD evidence also highlights the importance of paying attention to the **human and financial resources** required to create an agile administration, and to the mechanisms and instruments **for monitoring policy development and performance**, including the possibility to make corrections to courses of action if they are achieving results sub-optimally. Governments that develop and deploy these tools and practices in a strategic and integrated way, and consider the different complementarities across these tools of sound public governance when doing so, can enhance the quality and impact of policies and services.

Successful policy implementation is also predicated on an acknowledgement that this process involves technical as well as political implications. The public sector generally, and national governments in particular, no longer detain a monopoly on policy implementation. Different agencies and levels of government can be involved in the implementation of policies and initiatives, representing diverse and often conflicting interests. Indeed in many cases, policies are not implemented by those who design it, and sometimes they are pursued by actors or stakeholders from outside the public administration.

The first section of this chapter explores the role and importance of 1) **civil service leadership and skills, 2) digital tools, 3) public procurement, 4) Public-Private partnerships and public-civil partnerships, 5) Agile and innovative approaches to policy and service delivery, and 6) A strategic approach to policy and service delivery**. The chapter then highlights the need to engage in **7) monitoring** as a key component of sound policy implementation.

## Managing implementation

### *Public service leadership and skills for implementation*

Whatever the public policy may be, whether in health, education, finance, or science, civil servants lie at the core of its implementation. However, public services face new challenges to which they must respond effectively while at the same time deliver stable trustworthy and reliable services in a fair and timely manner (OECD, 2019[9]) . The OECD experience in public employment and management underscores the importance of developing adequate frameworks to strengthen the capacities and skills of the public sector in order to create a values-driven, trusted and capable, responsive and adaptive public service. Governments should build a proactive and innovative public service that integrates a long-term perspective in policy design and services. Possible measures include ensuring a balance of employment continuity and mobility to support policy implementation beyond a policy cycle, and investing in foresight and innovation.

The values that a system adopts depend on each country. As discussed in Chapter 1, public-governance values can include integrity openness, inclusiveness and accountability; as well as other such as agility, responsiveness and effectiveness. Adherence and compliance with these values is, for instance, fundamental to prevent corruption and misuse of public resources during the implementation process. The promotion of values across the public sector and at all levels of government can be supported by (i) proactive clarification and communication, (ii) leadership commitment, (iii) regular opportunities for all public servants to discuss and evaluate the value performance, (OECD, 2019[9]) and (iv) engagement of all – public servants and employees of partner organisations, specially through non-monetary incentives.

The quality of public policy implementation invariably depends on the capacities and motivation of the senior civil service to translate the policy decisions taken by the political leadership into manageable, actionable initiatives and to harness the necessary human and financial resources to implement them by ensuring that these initiatives are pursued successfully. To this end, the OECD recommends that senior-level public servants be appointed as a result of a competitive, merit-based process with the expectation that they will be able to provide impartial, evidence-informed advice. Employee training and development is at the core of any skills strategy, and is particularly important in civil services due to lower overall turnover (OECD, 2017[49]). Following the 2008 financial crisis however, training budgets were one of the first things to be cut, risking stifling civil service's ability to refresh the skills needed to implement new services. Resource scarcity is therefore one of the greatest obstacles for states seeking to improve policy implementation. Embedding leaning in the organisational culture and reinvesting in training programmes is thus crucial.

OECD evidence also suggests a set of civil servants' skills for effective policy implementation, which complement those required to pursue effective problem identification and policy design (OECD, 2017[49]):

- Skills to work in collaborative partnerships and networks to create better service delivery;
- Skills to commission and contract services, as in most cases, policies are not implemented by those who design it and often they are carried out by organisations outside the public administration.
- Skills to identify and address policy complementarities or contradictions in order to identify potential policy trade-off, resource-allocation and sequencing issues to ensure effective planning and implementation skills to make use of and maximize potential of the digital transformation.

This last point is particularly important as it is linked to the opportunities and challenges posed by digitalisation, and therefore with the need for governments to develop broader digital government strategies.

### Better service design and delivery through digital government

As described in chapter 3, the development of digital government strategies can be pivotal for the improvement of policy-making in all its stages, as it can be used strategically to shape public-governance outcomes beyond using them simply to improve government processes.

The diffusion and adoption of new digital technologies has altered citizens' expectations regarding the governments' ability to deliver public services, which respond to their needs. These new expectations present a challenge to governments, as it requires the digital transformation of the government itself. Failure adapt risks undermining the relationship between citizens and the government at the core of the social contract. In other words, the new dynamics generated by the digital age require a strategic approach to the design and delivery of public services that includes, among other things, digital government. Indeed, digital government can reduce administrative burden by decreasing the cost of compliance with government regulations and procedures. Business processes re-design is another means for governments to adapt to the rapidly evolving dynamics and relations between stakeholders in the new digital environment. To better shape public-governance outcomes and public service delivery, the OECD recommendation on Digital Government Strategies (2014[31]) recommends conducting early sharing, testing and evaluation of prototypes with the involvement of expected end-users, as well as ensuring the availability of a comprehensive picture of on-going digital initiatives to avoid duplication of systems and datasets. This requires a commitment to the practices emphasised in section 2.4 as part of the enabler "Change management and innovation". The *OECD Recommendation on Digital Government Strategies* (2014[31]) [OECD/LEGAL/0406] codifies best practice on the adoption of "more effective co-ordination mechanisms, stronger capacities and framework conditions to improve digital technologies' effectiveness for delivering public value and strengthening citizen trust" and on the strategic use of data across the public sector. The *Recommendation on Digital Government Strategies* advises governments to:

- Enhance the value of data in improving the quality of public services and citizen well-being (Principle 3)
- Ensure coherent use of digital technologies across policy areas and levels of government (Principle 6)
- Develop clear business cases to sustain the funding and focused implementation of digital technologies project (Principle 9)
- Reinforce institutional capacities to manage and monitor projects' implementation (Principle 10)
- Procure digital technologies based on assessment of existing assets (Principle 11).

While digital government is not a separate target of the 2030 Agenda, digital technologies can be both a lever and accelerator in achieving the SDGs (OECD, 2019[47]). In particular, digital technologies can be strategically used to develop collaborative approaches to implement the SDGs.

---

### Box 4.1. ChileAtiende

ChileAtiende seeks to bring the State closer to its citizen, by providing a multichannel and multiservice network for the delivery of public services (one-stop shop). The network includes the following channels:

- Offices geographically distributed across the country to cover most of the population;
- Digital Channel: a website that provides information on more than 2,500 benefits and services in simple citizen language;
- Call Center: provides information and orientation on public services and benefits and
- ChileAtiende Vehicles: vans that reach remote and rural areas to provide public services.

The project was launched in January 2012. It was inspired by the compared experiences of Canada, Singapore and Australia, and designed by seizing an opportunity to reuse previously installed capacities

Source: (OECD[58]) Digital Government Toolkit (http://www.oecd.org/governance/digital-government/toolkit/home/ ). This toolkit is designed to help governments in the implementation of the OECD Recommendation on Digital Government Strategies. By comparing good practices across OECD Member countries, this site can guide decision-makers in using digital technologies to encourage innovation, transparency, and efficiency in the public sector.

---

### *Public Procurement as a strategic lever to pursue policy objectives*

Policymakers can use public procurement as a strategic lever to pursue policy objectives: "well-designed public procurement systems contribute to achieving pressing policy goals such as environmental protection, innovation, job creation and the development of small and medium enterprises" (OECD, 2015[59]). In Australia for instance, the Indigenous Procurement Policy has become an incredibly effective lever to drive Indigenous economic development (see Box 4.2).

Box 4.2. Australia's Indigenous Procurement Policy

The Indigenous Procurement Policy (IPP) is a mandated procurement-connected policy of the Australian Government's Commonwealth Procurement Rules. It allows Australian Government buyers to purchase directly from indigenous small and medium enterprises (SMEs) through a simplified, yet efficient, quote process. The IPP aims to increase the rate of purchasing thereby helping to drive indigenous economic development and entrepreneurship.

To achieve these objectives, the IPP has three main components:

- Annual targets for the number of contract awarded to indigenous businesses;
- A Mandatory Set-Aside (MSA) for remote contracts and those valued between AUD 80 000 and AUD 200 000;
- Minimum indigenous participation requirements in contracts valued at or above AUD 7.5 Million in selected industries, known as the Mandatory Minimum Requirements (MMR).

In 2013, a reported AUD 6 Million in Commonwealth contracts were awarded to fewer than 30 indigenous businesses. Since the IPP's introduction in 2015, over 1 550 indigenous businesses have won 13 700 contracts valued at AUD 2.2 Billion.

Source: Example of country practice provided by the Government of Australia as part of the Policy Framework's consultation process

In particular, governments are increasingly using public procurement as a policy lever to support broader outcomes consistent with SDGs. To this end, the *OECD Recommendation on Public Procurement* (2015[59]) [OECD/LEGAL/0411] recommends that governments:

- Evaluate the use of public procurement as one method of pursuing secondary policy objectives in accordance with clear national priorities;
- Develop an appropriate strategy for the integration of secondary policy objectives in public procurement systems;
- Employ an appropriate impact assessment methodology to measure the effectiveness of procurement in achieving secondary policy objectives.

### Public-Private partnerships (PPPs) and public-civil partnerships

Contracts are governance instruments commonly used to improve policy implementation (OECD, 2007[81]). They allow for the sharing of policy implementation functions with other levels of governments and with actors such as the private sector. One key contractual arrangement are Public-Private Partnerships (PPPs). PPPs are "long term agreements between the government and a private partner whereby the private partner delivers and funds public services using a capital asset, sharing the associated risks. PPPs may deliver public services both with regard to infrastructure assets (such as bridges, roads) and social assets (such as hospitals, utilities, prisons)." In this regard, the *OECD Recommendation on Principles for Public Governance of Public-Private Partnerships* (2012[82]) [OECD/LEGAL/0392] provides guidance on such partnerships' three main objectives:

- Establish a clear, predictable and legitimate institutional framework supported by competent and well-resourced authorities.
- Ground the selection of Public-Private Partnerships in value for money.

- Use the budgetary process transparently to minimise fiscal risks and ensure the integrity of the procurement process.
- Contracts for sharing policy implementation functions can also be established with non-private actors such as associations, civil society organisations or local communities. Such public-civil partnerships can enable direct stakeholder participation in service design, delivery and management of resources and commons.

### Agile and innovative approaches to policy and service delivery

As mentioned throughout this Framework, innovation is critical to find new solutions and approaches to deal with complexity. Given the dynamic policy environment that countries are facing, governments are approaching policy implementation and service delivery from an innovative and agile approach, for instance through the incorporation of early feedback loops during the implementation process (OECD, 2019[72]).

Agile project management methodologies focus on principles such as simplicity, quick iteration, and close customer collaboration. Agile approaches based on collaboration, for instance between civil servants responsible for planning the delivery of a policy or service and potential users, allow for regular interactions to discuss progress and feedback.

Moreover, processes for agile policy implementation and service delivery can include practices such as early prototyping and user testing (OECD, 2017[73]), with the goal to create a regular feedback loop that enables continuous improvements during the implementation process. According to the OECD Observatory of Public Sector Innovation (2019), some examples of agile and/or innovative approaches for implementation and delivery are:

- *Toolkits and implementation guidance documents*, including easily updatable implementation guidelines and online discussion forums;
- *Project management tools*, such as a results frameworks, critical path analysis, Gantt charts and Kanban board;
- *Crowdsourcing*; as a tool to capitalise though online communities large audience, process data and information quickly, with quality control, and accomplish tasks that might have traditionally given to small groups.
- *Digital networks and communities of practice*, across the civil service, particular important to scaling up projects from piloting to broader implementation.
- *Co-creation, co-production and co-delivery*, to engage many users in creating innovative solutions as a way to build ownership and secure greater tolerance for eventual setbacks.
- *Innovation Labs and units*, which can facilitate a project-based approach for innovation and implementation, "providing rooms to develop new ways of doing things".
- *Behavioural insight methods* as an "inductive approach to the design and delivery of policies, that is driven by experimentation and piloting, seeking to understand the actual behaviour of the beneficiaries of policies and testing possible solutions before implementation" (OECD, 2019[74])
- *User-centric design methods*, which are increasingly being applied to public service delivery, can help government officials to understand how people interact with systems and processes, and to view citizens holistically, and recognise that each individual has specific wants and needs(OECD, 2017[75]) .
- *Blameless retrospectives*, as a method to discuss among the implementation team, in an open and honest way, about how the policy/project has worked.

## *A strategic approach to the implementation of the SDGs*

The implementation of the United Nations Sustainable Development Goals (SDGs) represents a significant challenge for all countries irrespective of income levels. To deliver on the 2030 Agenda, governments need to find new ways to co-ordinate, consult and work across institutions and policy areas (OECD, 2019[47]). To overcome the governance challenges the implementation of the SDGs poses, governments need to make strategic use of policy instruments such as the budget, procurement and regulatory policy. This also implies the design and implementation of innovative, forward-looking policies and programmes (OECD, 2019[47]).

Since 2015, many countries have started to incorporate and reflect the SDGs in their policy documents. However, even if we see countries including the SDGs in strategic documents, governments will need to build additional capacities to integrate the SDGs into their day-to-day management systems to fully mainstream the SDGs across the public administration and successfully implement them. While some countries are making significant progress in this regard, this is not yet happening everywhere. The Secretariat has found that in OECD countries, the SDGs are often integrated into a national performance framework (71%) but less so within national budget systems (45%). Integration therefore is more alignment than actual integration. SDGs become one framework among others rather than a coherent strategy that can change mind-sets and working methods (2018[53]). The national budget-setting and implementation process can be used to improve the pursuit of the SDGs:

- If budget documents adequately reflect which policy objectives are prioritised and how the effective allocation of resources can support their pursuit, measuring the performance of implementing the SDGs can eventually be improved.
- Through multi-year budget frameworks, governments can also effectively promote policy integration. Policymakers can ensure that policy objectives are not only pursued over the short- and medium-term but over the longer term beyond electoral cycle using multi-year budget forecasting and planning frameworks.
- Recently, countries across the OECD and beyond have also started to use public procurement strategies to ensure that purchases of goods, services and works by governments and state-owned enterprises align with the pursuit of the SDGs.

Through whole-of-government coordination and a focus on policy coherence, governments can further guarantee an integrated approach to SDG implementation:

- Due to the integrated character of the 2030 Agenda, governments need to overcome policy silos and create long-term objectives that connect different policy sectors and areas. A whole-of-government approach is particularly important for implementation.
- Given the broad scope of the SDGs and the incentive for some stakeholders to cherry-pick the easiest and less costly areas to implement, solid policy co-ordination, especially from the Centre-of-Government is crucial to guarantee policy coherence and to overcome the complex policy challenges the SDGs represent (OECD, 2019[47]) .
- According to UNDESA and UN CEPA, coordination by the CoG is one of the most important strategies to ensure an integrated approach to SDG implementation (United Nations, 2018[6]).

In order to examine how policies and allocated resources for the implementation of the SDGs achieve their purpose, monitoring and evaluation (M&E) represent important tools at the disposal of policymakers (evaluation is discussed in greater detail in Chapter 5). They take on particular importance due to the SDGs' complex and inter-connected character. Robust M&E is an important tool to:

- Identify implementation barriers;
- Strengthen the links between short-term programmes and policies and strategic outcomes; and

- Communicate to the general public and civil society if (and how) the government is progressing toward the achievement of the different SDG targets.

Nevertheless, several challenges remain, for instance regarding the government's capacity to gather solid data in a resource-effective way and to guarantee that information collected is managed effectively. Moreover, governments need to find new ways to publish relevant information and engage with key stakeholders outside of government (e.g. citizens, NGOs, Parliament etc.) on performance with regard to the SDGs (OECD, 2019[47]).

## Core questions for consideration

- Does the government proactively promote and support values of sound civil service management – such as codes of conduct- to specifically address corruption and misuse of public resources during the implementation process?

- Does your government has a strategy to use digital technologies – back-office and front-office - in a coherent and integrated way to shape public policy implementation in all policy domains and across all levels of government?

- Do your government procurement systems establish mechanisms to enhance transparency? Does your government envisage e-procurement modalities?

- Has your government actively – and explicitly – encouraged the adoption of innovative and agile approaches to policy implementation and service delivery?

- Has your government mandated a core institution to lead the process of integrating the SDGs into national strategic policy-setting, implementation, evaluation and reporting on progress? Does the institution ensure that the national strategy to pursuing the SDGs reflects specific regional circumstances across the country?

- Does your government have in place robust mechanisms to coordinate across policy areas and administrative units and does it generate incentives to promote co-ordination across ministries and agencies for pursuing the SDGs, such as financial, or individual or collective performance targets?

- Are there regular assessments to identify and assess potential positive and negative impacts of policy proposals and regulations on sustainable development?

## Monitoring performance

Performance monitoring is "the continuous function that uses systematic collection of data on specified indicators to provide management and the main stakeholders of an ongoing policy or reform initiative with indications of the extent of progress and achievement of objectives and progress in the use of allocated funds" (OECD, 2016[23]). It is a critical tool to inform governments on how they are progressing along the path to achieving their stated policy goals.

Monitoring policy and governance performance is essential to ensure the proper implementation of a public policy. Unlike policy evaluation, which seeks to analyse the implementation of an intervention for its impact on results and outcomes (see chapter 5), monitoring is mainly a descriptive tool that helps policymakers track progress and make adjustments when necessary during the implementation phase to make sure it is on track to achieve the objectives for which it was adopted. Linkages between the government's strategic objectives, public spending and clear performance goals carry added importance as governments pursue the translation of Agenda 2030 in their national contexts (OECD, 2019[47]). This can potentially help governments assess how their decisions are promoting the SDGs in a way that is coherent with national priorities. Policy monitoring information can feed **planning, decision-making and improve performance**, for example by "the analysis of data on the policy context, problems or needs in the preparation of a policy intervention, decisions on the allocation of resources and/or the choice between different options" (OECD, 2017[59]). It can moreover serve as a **follow-up tool**, improving the implementation processes and the functioning of organisations; with a view to further enhance efficiency or the use of organisational capacity, among others. Eventually, it **provides accountability to stakeholders**, on issues such as the use of resources, internal processes, and the outputs and outcomes of a policy (OECD, 2017[59]).

Over the long term, data and information accumulated during implementation through monitoring can supplement evaluation insights and, together with evaluation (discussed in the next chapter), can inform **formulation and decision-making** of other policy interventions, for instance as part of performance-informed budgeting. Policy monitoring can be used to identify areas for further investigation and evaluation, as a basis for data-driven reviews in which qualitative discussions help to provide context for progress on indicators, which in turn allows organisations to adjust existing Key Performance Indicators (KPIs) or to set new ones.

Regardless of the policy or governance area, policymakers have to decide what elements should be monitored and how these can be tracked. In this regard, the OECD and the European Union, through the joint SIGMA initiative that provides advice based on the experience of EU and OECD member states, have defined *Public Administration Principles* that include advice for purposeful monitoring (SIGMA, 2017[5]). Governments could therefore:

- Set reform objectives and targets in planning documents.
- Define a set of performance indicators (aligned with objectives) that monitor progress on the implementation of reforms in planning documents.
- Ensure that performance indicators are measurable and relevant to the objectives and support accountability arrangements between institutions and responsible managers.
- Establish a data-collection system for all identified indicators that provides ministers and officials with timely and accurate data.
- Conduct progress reports at least every two years and ensure that they are publicly available and form a basis for discussion of implementation at political and top administrative levels.
- Put in place functioning central steering and strategy review processes. Involve civil society and the business community in the monitoring and review process by ensuring transparency and access to information, and enable them to provide input on implementation performance and challenges.

Social participation oversight and oversight mechanisms by civil society can play an important role in monitoring. The OECD *Recommendation of the Council on Public Integrity* (2017[11]) [OECD/LEGAL/0435] highlights the role of "watchdog" organisations, citizens groups, labour unions and independent media in ensuring accountability.

A good monitoring system relies on comprehensive, quality data. As such, a high quality national statistics system is an integral part of any monitoring strategy, as well as up-to-date databases and registers that mutually communicate and disaggregate data at the desired level. In recent years, a number of more forward looking monitoring practices that use data-driven public sector approaches have emerged. Data-driven public sector (DDPS) is one of the six dimensions of the OECD *Recommendation on Digital Government Strategies* (2014[31]) [OECD/LEGAL/0406], which highlights the importance of data as a foundational enabler in the public sector working together to forecast needs, shape delivery and understand and respond to change. According to the OECD Report *The Path to Becoming a Data-Driven Public Sector* (OECD, 2019[60]), in the context of monitoring, DDPS generates an environment in which data about policy interventions is available in real time. Decision makers can thus avoid waiting for monthly or quarterly updates across a wide range of policy areas because the data they need is more frequently available and accessible. As a result, governments can gain better insights into the policy process and make quick policy adjustments in the short-term, with benefits in the mid-and long-term.

### Monitoring government-wide policy priorities

Monitoring government-wide policy priorities has become one of the Centre-of-Government's (CoG) major responsibilities to ensure that operational and strategic objectives are reached and policies are implemented in an effective and co-ordinated manner (OECD, 2018[32]).

In this regard, as highlighted in Chapter 2, the CoG in OECD Member countries is increasingly focusing on monitoring the alignment of policies as well as their impact, in order to improve co-ordination across multidimensional policies and highlight progress and achievements vis-à-vis stakeholders.

The 2017 *OECD Survey on the Organisation and Functions of the CoG* showed that the above mentioned monitoring tasks are increasingly fulfilled by special monitoring units, namely results and delivery units, government project units, or government co-ordination units with different capacities (OECD, 2018[32]). Delivery Units (DUs), for instance, aim help line ministries with collecting data for different policy priorities, identifying all components of the implementation process, and offer support with the definition of Key Performance Indicators and policy targets that link performance information across related single- and multi-sector strategies. Nevertheless, DU and the *deliverology* approach have their limits. Indeed, without the appropriate political backing, a clearly defined mission and an effective mechanism for adjusting expectations, DUs can produce mixed results (Gold, 2017[61]).

While DUs can be a useful strategic tool, they must adopt a whole-of-government approach to monitoring and evaluating policy performance. In order to link policies with the delivery of desired outcomes, Key Performance Indicators (KPIs) are composite by definition, and need to cover a mix of input, intermediate (process, output) and outcome indicators. DUs and KPIs need to be carefully adapted to the institutional framework within a country in order to optimise their utility over time

### Monitoring financial performance and budget execution

OECD Member countries have developed different monitoring capacities to ensure efficient policy-making. The monitoring of the administration's financial performance and budget execution can help governments to assess the effectiveness of public spending against their strategic objectives and adjust the allocation of financial resources in case of unforeseen implementation challenges or misspending. To this effect, clear performance goals as well as sufficient control mechanisms should be established, to allow senior civil servants to track the performance. Linkages between the government's strategic objectives (as identified for example in its multi-year development planning) and its spending results areas in the national budget need to be clearly identified.

These links take on added importance as governments pursue the translation of the UN SDGs into their national contexts through a triangulation exercise that aligns the SDGs with national strategic planning objectives and spending result areas in the national budget (OECD, 2019[47]). Governments can then align their national strategic objectives (now reflecting the SDGs) with the spending result areas in the national budget. This has the potential of enabling governments to assess how their financial allocations and spending decisions are advancing the country down the path of achieving the SDGs in a way that reflects national development priorities and objectives.

The *OECD Recommendation on Budgetary Governance* (2015[48]) [OECD/LEGAL/0410] advises governments on to "actively plan, manage and monitor the execution of the budget" and to ensure that performance is integral to the budget process. To that end, the *Recommendation on Budgetary Governance* recommends that Adherents use "performance information that is:

- limited to a small number of relevant indicators for each policy programme or area;
- clear and easily understood;
- clearly linked to government-wide strategic objectives;

- functional for tracking of results against targets and for comparison with international and other benchmarks."

Additionally, the *OECD Recommendation on Budgetary Governance* (OECD, 2015[48]) [OECD/LEGAL/0410] recommends that governments "provides for an inclusive, participative and realistic debate on budgetary choices, by facilitating the engagement of parliaments, citizens and civil society organisations". Citizens can also play a role in monitoring budget execution. To this end, the OECD Budget Transparency Toolkit suggests 1) Making the budget information accessible to the public, 2) Using open data to support budget transparency, 3) Making the budget more inclusive and participative (OECD, 2017[62]).

Moreover, countries could improve their monitoring efforts through, inter alia, developing oversight capacities in the Central Budget Authority and line ministries as appropriate and organise the national budget around composite, multidimensional result areas. Supreme Audit Institutions can also play an important role by conducting performance audits to inform decision-makers. This enables governments to measure the impact of spending decisions against the strategic outcomes identified in the national strategy (and in the SDGs).

### *Measuring regulatory performance and ensuring implementation*

In many OECD Member countries, measuring regulatory performance is a tool to improve policy-making and service delivery, as it can help governments to identify specific barriers and improve regulations in general, and also in specific sectors, for instance, to reduce compliance costs, to maximize net benefits and to ensure that regulations are transparent and accessible for citizens (see chapter 3). Moreover, intermediate successes can be measured and directly communicated as part of the implementation process. The *OECD Recommendation on Regulatory Policy and Governance* (2012[27]) [OECD/LEGAL/0390] recommends that Adherents "establish mechanisms and institutions to actively provide oversight of regulatory policy procedures and goals, support and implement regulatory policy, and thereby foster regulatory quality".

Improving the implementation and the enforcement of regulations is a shared challenge across OECD Member countries (OECD, 2018[63]). Historically, this has been an underdeveloped area of research, despite the key role proper enforcement of regulations plays in people's lives.

One of the most important ways to enforce regulations and to ensure regulatory compliance is through inspections. The way these are planned, targeted, and communicated, and the ethical standards and independence that govern how inspectors carry out their mandate are key factors that governments could consider to ensure that regulations are implemented effectively. In this connection, the Secretariat has developed eleven principles "on which effective and efficient regulatory enforcement and inspections should be based in pursuit of the best compliance outcomes and highest regulatory quality" (OECD, 2014[64]):

- *Evidence-based enforcement*. Deciding what to inspect and how should be grounded on data and evidence, and results should be evaluated regularly.
- *Selectivity*. Promoting compliance and enforcing rules should be left to market forces, private sector and civil society actions wherever possible
- *Risk focus and proportionality*. Enforcement needs to be risk-based and proportionate.
- *Responsive regulation*. Inspection enforcement actions should be modulated depending on the profile and behaviour of specific businesses.
- *Long-term vision*. Governments should adopt policies and institutional mechanisms on regulatory enforcement and inspections with clear objectives and a long-term road-map.

- *Co-ordination and consolidation.* Less duplication and overlaps will ensure better use of public resources, minimise burden on regulated subjects, and maximise effectiveness.
- *Transparent governance.* Governance structures and human resources policies for regulatory enforcement should support transparency, professionalism, and results oriented management.
- *Information integration.* Information and communication technologies should be used to maximise risk-focus, co-ordination and information-sharing – as well as optimal use of resources.
- *Clear and fair process.* Coherent legislation to organise inspections and enforcement needs to be adopted and published, and clearly articulate rights and obligations of officials and of businesses.
- *Compliance promotion.* Transparency and compliance should be promoted through the use of appropriate instruments such as guidance, toolkits and checklists.
- *Professionalism.* Inspectors should be trained and managed to ensure professionalism, integrity, consistency and transparency.

### Building robust governance indicators

As mentioned above, performance indicators are central for governments to measure progress in achieving national strategic sustainable development goals. Some of these indicators can measure the impact of governance reforms on improving the government's capacity to pursue its development goals for the country. In particular, translating the SDGs into national goals with robust governance indicators can allow the government to reflect the SDGs in their strategic plans (OECD, 2019[47]). Policymakers have continuously to decide what elements of a policy should be monitored and how these can be tracked through various different indicators. Many OECD Member countries use indicators that comply with the SMART criteria - criteria that are sufficiently specific, measurable, attainable, relevant, and time bound. A typology of governance indicators can distinguish between:

- *Input indicators*: measure the quantity and type of resources, such as staff, money, time, equipment, etc. the Government invests to attain a specific public policy.
- *Process indicators*: refer to actual processes employed, often with assessment of the effectiveness from individuals involved in the policy.
- *Output indicators*: refer to the quantity, type and quality of goods or services produced by the Government's policy. They can include operational goals such as the number of meetings held.
- *Outcome/Impact indicators*: measure the strategic effect and change produced by the policy implemented. Outcome indicators commonly refer to short-term or immediate effect, while impact indicators refer to long-term effect.

Box 4.3. Toward a framework to assessing the relevance and robustness of public governance indicators

Based on the worked carried out by the OECD in governance indicators, Lafortune et al (2017) have proposed criteria to evaluate the relevance and robustness of public governance indicators.

*Relevance* corresponds to the degree to which indicators serve a clear purpose and provide useful information that can guide public sector reforms. The target audience of these indicators are mainly decision makers. To be useful and relevant is fundamental that the indicators sets provided are:

*Action worthy*; an indicators should measure something that is important and which is meaningful for policymakers and the society.

*Actionability*; governments should know what actions they need to take in order to improve their performance. Indicators should provide useful and informative insights into the type of reform countries should engage.

*Behavioural*; while measuring the existence of directives, laws and other institutional documents, provided some information on the legal framework in place, what really matters is that they are actually implemented (output) and what their outcome/impact is. Therefore, in order to effectively inform public sector reforms, indicators should generally measure actual and observable facts, practices, and implementation (de facto).

*Robustness* corresponds to the statistical soundness of indicators. In this regard, the authors outline two main characteristics:

*Validity*: A valid indicator measures precisely the concept it is intended to measure.

*Reliability*. The measure should produce consistent results when repeated across populations and settings and event when assessed by different peoples and different times. In this regard, does the indicator provide stable results across various population and circumstances?

Source: Lafortune, G., Gonzalez, S., and Lonti, Z. (2018[65]), Government at a Glance: A Dashboard Approach to Indicators. The Palgrave Handbook of Indicators of Global Governance, Palgrave Macmillan, Cham.

Box 4.4. The German Sustainable Development Strategy

The German Sustainable Development Strategy (GSDS) emerged in 2016 and allows the German government to track its progress towards implementing the UN 2030 Agenda. The strategy is composed of a set of 66 national targets and indicators which cover all 17 SDGs and fulfil the Public Administration Principles defined by the SIGMA initiative.

The Federal Statistical Office conducts a biennial Indicator Report that analyses the status of the targets and illustrates the result with a weather symbol. The reports are publicly available and generate substantial awareness and discussion among the broader public.

Source: Example of country practice provided by the Government of Germany as part of the Policy Framework's consultation process

How governments make strategic use of policy evaluation to assess the relevance and fulfilment of objectives, efficiency, effectiveness, impact and sustainability of policies to foster a range of governance objectives will be discussed in Chapter 5.

## Core questions for consideration

- Has your government developed specific initiatives to ensure that performance information and data feed a strategic monitoring mechanism?
- Is your government focusing on translating the UN SDGs into national planning? Is the government aligning its national strategic planning goals as they reflect the SDGs with spending result areas in the national budget in a way that will enable it to measure the impact of spending on the pursuit of its planning objectives in the context of its efforts to implement the SDGs?
- How are monitoring results used to improve decision-making, including allowing senior civil servants to track financial performance and budget execution and link this performance to the pursuit of the strategies the budget is funding?
- Are the necessary mechanisms in place to ensure regulatory compliance and monitor regulatory enforcement against outcomes?
- Does transparency and access to public information mechanisms play a role in monitoring performance?
- Is the monitoring aspect of a policy or regulation systematically considered at the time of policy formulation?

## Additional resources:

OECD legal instruments:

- OECD Recommendation of the Council on Public Procurement (2015) [OECD/LEGAL/0411]
- OECD Recommendation of the Council on Digital Government Strategies (2014) [OECD/LEGAL/0406]
- OECD Recommendation of the Council on Public Service Leadership and Capability (2019) [OECD/LEGAL/0445]
- OECD Recommendation on Principles for Public Governance of Public-Private Partnerships [OECD/LEGAL/0392]
- OECD Recommendation on Budgetary Governance (2015) [OECD/LEGAL/0410]
- OECD Recommendation on Regulatory Policy and Governance (2012) [OECD/LEGAL/0390]

Other relevant OECD tools:

- OECD Toolkit Navigator (web resource)
- OECD Delivering Better Policies Through Behavioural Insights: New Approaches, (2019)
- OECD Embracing Innovation in Government: Global Trends (2018)
- OECD Framework for the Governance of Infrastructure (2017)
- OECD Public Governance Review: Skills for a High Performing Civil Service (2017)
- OECD Comparative Study: Digital Government Strategies for Transforming Public Services in the Welfare Areas (2016)
- OECD Public Procurement Toolbox (2016)

- OECD Centre Stage, Driving Better Policies from the Centre of Government (2014)OECD Regulatory Enforcement and Inspections Toolkit (2018)
- OECD Regulatory Enforcement and Inspections, OECD Best Practice Principles for Regulatory Policy (2014)
- SIGMA Principles of Public Administration (2017)

## References

Gold, J. (2017), Tracking delivery Global trends and warning signs in delivery units, Institute for Government, London. [61]

Lafortune, G., S. Gonzalez and Z. Lonti (2018), "Government at a Glance: A Dashboard Approach to Indicators", in The Palgrave Handbook of Indicators in Global Governance, Springer International Publishing, http://dx.doi.org/10.1007/978-3-319-62707-6_9. [65]

OECD Digital Government Toolkit - Organisation for Economic Co-operation and Development, https://www.oecd.org/governance/digital-government/toolkit/ (accessed on 7 October 2019). [58]

OECD (2019), The Path to Becoming a Data-Driven Public Sector, OECD Digital Government Studies, OECD Publishing, Paris, https://doi.org/10.1787/059814a7-en. [60]

OECD (2019), Governance as an SDG Accelerator : Country Experiences and Tools, OECD Publishing, Paris, https://dx.doi.org/10.1787/0666b085-en. [47]

OECD (2019), How do we Make it Happen?: Implementing Public Sector Innovation, Observatory of Public Sector Innovation, OECD Publishing, Paris [72]

OECD (2019), Delivering Better Policies Through Behavioural Insights: New Approaches, OECD Publishing, Paris, https://dx.doi.org/10.1787/6c9291e2-en. [74]

OECD (2019), Recommendation of the Council on Public Service Leadership and Capability. [9]

OECD (2018), Centre Stage 2, OECD Centres of Government. [32]

OECD (2018), OECD Regulatory Enforcement and Inspections Toolkit, OECD Publishing, Paris, https://dx.doi.org/10.1787/9789264303959-en. [63]

OECD (2017), Budget Transparency Toolkit, http://www.oecd.org/gov/budgeting/Budgeting-Transparency-Toolkit.pdf (accessed on 7 October 2019). [62]

OECD (2017), Towards Open Government Indicators: Framework for the Govenrance of Open Government (GOOG) index and the checklist for open government impact indictors, concept note, non-published. [59]

OECD (2017), Embracing Innovation in Government Global Trends. OECD Publishing, Paris. [75]

OECD (2017), Fostering Innovation in the Public Sector, OECD Publishing, Paris, https://dx.doi.org/10.1787/9789264270879-en. [73]

OECD (2017), Skills for a High Performing Civil Service, OECD Publishing, Paris. [49]

OECD (2016), Open Government:The global context and the way forward. [23]

OECD (2015), Recommendation of the Council on Budgetary Governance.    [48]

OECD (2015), *Recommendation of the Council on Public Procurement.*    [59]

OECD (2014), Recommendation of the Council on Digital Government Strategies.    [31]

OECD (2014), Regulatory Enforcement and Inspections, OECD Best Practice Principles for Regulatory Policy, OECD Publishing, Paris, https://dx.doi.org/10.1787/9789264208117-en.    [64]

OECD (2012), Recommendation of the Council on Regulatory Policy and Governance, http://www.oecd.org/regreform (accessed on 4 October 2019).    [27]

OECD (2012), Recommendation of the Council on Principles for Public Governance of Public-Private Partnerships.    [82]

SIGMA (2017), The Principles of Public Administration 2017 edition, http://www.oecd.org/termsandconditions. (accessed on 4 October 2019).    [5]

United Nations (2018), Principles of effective governance for sustainable development, Economic and Social Council, Official Recors 2018, Supplement No. 24, E/2018/44-E/C.16/2018/8, para. 3.    [6]

# 5 Toward robust policy evaluation

This chapter discusses the importance of policy evaluation, and provides tools and strategies to promote and produce high quality evaluations. As distinguished from policy monitoring, policy evaluation seeks to analyse linkages between policy interventions and effects. Policy evaluations can therefore enhance the quality of decision-making and provide tailored advice to improve policy formulation and implementation. Despite these findings, evidence collected by the OECD suggests that, regardless of strong commitments, policy evaluation often constitutes the weakest link in the policy cycle and countries are still facing substantial challenges to promote policy evaluation. The first section of this chapter provides guidance on how to build an institutional framework and promote the quality and use of evaluations in policy-making. The following section highlights the need to review the effect of regulations.

Evaluating performance and results helps to understand better why some policies work and others do not. By producing, using and promoting evidence on policy performance, policy evaluation supports the quality of decision-making (see chapter 2), providing tailored advice to improve policy formulation (chapter 3) and implementation (chapter 4). Policy evaluation, along with other practices such as user and staff feedback built into policy implementation processes, enables the strategic use of **feedback loops in the policy-making process to improve policy performance**, as it connects policies outcomes, impacts, and policymakers' decisions (learning dimension), as well as government and beneficiaries (stronger focus on the accountability dimension).

Policy evaluation is the structured and objective assessment of an ongoing or completed policy or reform initiative. The aim is to determine, *inter alia*, the relevance and fulfilment of objectives along with the initiative's efficiency, effectiveness, impact and sustainability[1]. As distinguished from policy monitoring – which, as explained in chapter 4, is essentially a descriptive exercise – policy evaluation seeks to analyse linkages between policy interventions and effects. It strives to create deeper understanding of observed policy success or failure as an end in itself and as a means to correct course and improve performance to enhance results and outcomes.

Robust policy-evaluation systems imply that evaluations are part and parcel of the policy cycle; that evaluations are carried out rigorously and systematically; that the results are used by decisions-makers; and that information is readily available to the public (Lázaro, 2015[66]). Moreover, evaluation methods need to be taking into account during the policy-formulation and design phase and integrated into an overall approach, in order to ensure that the necessary information and data required for effective policy evaluation can be collected during the implementation phase. Policy evaluation needs to be incorporated into the design of strategies for pursuing the SDGs (OECD, 2019[47]). Nevertheless few countries have established mechanisms to evaluate SDG achievements. Mainstreaming evaluation of the SDGs and Agenda 2030 therefore constitutes and important element on the policy-making agenda for all countries that are engaged in designing and pursuing the SDGs.

Given the overall importance and benefit of policy evaluation, several OECD Recommendations - such as the ones on *Open Government* and *Public Integrity* - underline the importance of undertaking evaluations. More specifically:

- The *Recommendation on Regulatory Policy and Governance* (OECD, 2012[27]) [OECD/LEGAL/0390] recommends that Adherents "[c]onduct systematic programme reviews of the stock of significant regulation against clearly defined policy goals, including consideration of costs and benefits, to ensure that regulations remain up to date, cost justified, cost effective and consistent, and deliver the intended policy objectives."

- The *Recommendation on Budgetary Governance* (OECD, 2015[48]) [OECD/LEGAL/0410] recommends that governments ensure that "performance, evaluation & value for money are integral to the budget process". To this end, the *Recommendation* suggests countries evaluate and review "expenditure programmes (including associated staffing resources as well as tax expenditures) in a manner that is objective, routine and regular, to inform resource allocation and re-prioritisation both within line ministries and across government as a whole".

Nevertheless, policy evaluation very often constitutes the weakest link in the policy cycle and countries are still facing substantial challenges to promote policy evaluation (see Figure 5.1).

## Figure 5.1. Government's current challenges for promoting policy evaluations

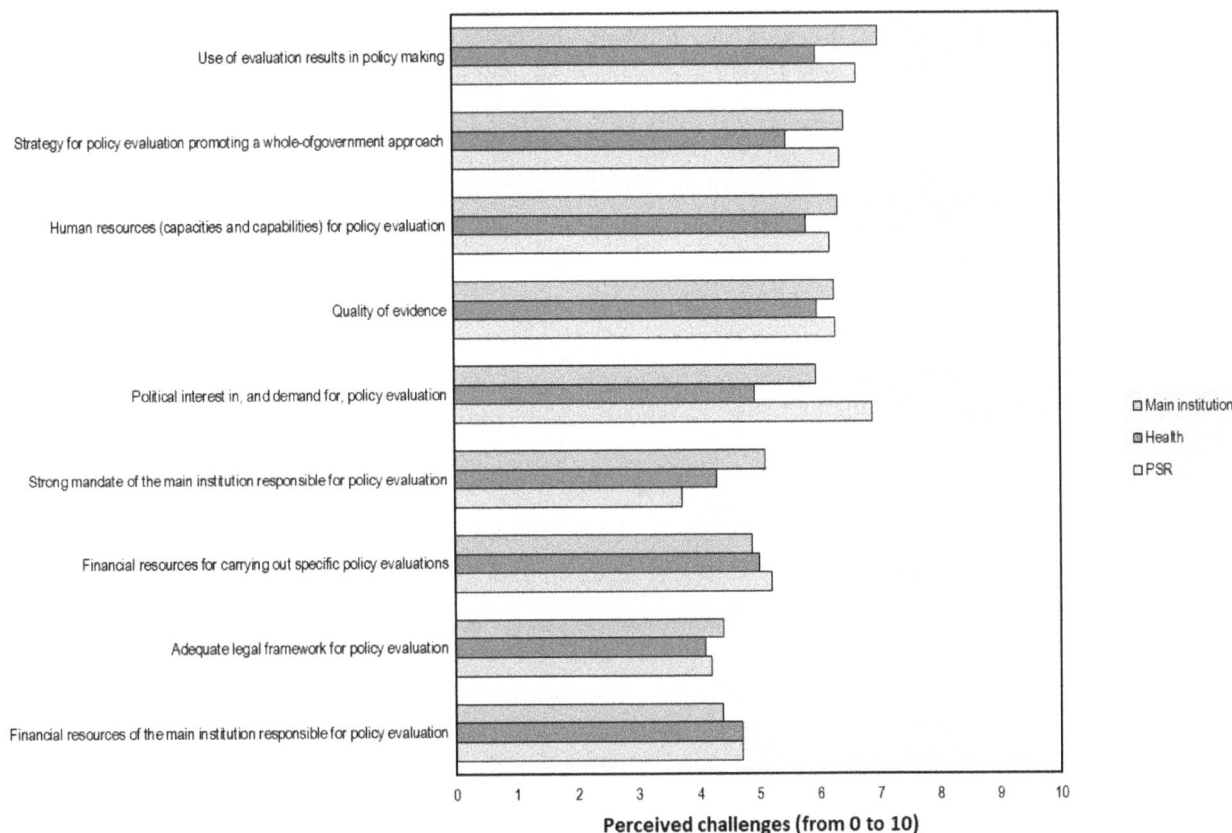

*Note*: For the main institution n=42 (35 OECD Member countries). For the Health ministries n=31 (28 OECD Member countries). 9 countries (7 OECD Member countries) did not participate on this survey. Moreover, 2 countries (1 OECD Member country) are not included as they answered that none of the policies that fall in their institution's responsibility are evaluated. For the PSR ministries n=25 (20 OECD Member countries). 11 countries (10 OECD Member countries) did not participate on this survey. Moreover, 6 countries (5 OECD Member countries) are not included as they answered that none of the policies that fall in their institution's responsibility are evaluated. Answers reflect responses to the questions, "What are the government's current challenges for promoting policy evaluations?" for the main institution and "What are current challenges for promoting policy evaluation in your institution?" for Health and PSR, where 0 indicates that is a "rare challenge", 5 is "Neutral", and 10 is a "principal challenge".
*Source*: OECD Survey on Policy Evaluation (2018[67])

As Figure 5.1 shows, developing and/or implementing a strategy for promoting a whole-of-government approach on policy evaluation is a key challenge for many countries. Such a strategy should ideally address two main issues, thus providing guidance on how to:

- **Build an institutional framework for policy evaluation,** which provides amongst others (a) the legal basis to undertake policy evaluations; (b) macro-level guidance on when and how to carry out evaluations; and (c) the identification of mandated institutional actors with allocated resources to oversee or carry out evaluations.

- Promote the **quality and use of policy evaluations** across government, including efforts related to building human resources capacity, ensuring appropriate stakeholder engagement, etc.

## Building an institutional framework for policy evaluation

As for any area of public governance, a fit-for-purpose adequate institutional framework constitutes a solid basis to embed the practice of evaluations across government in a systematic and systemic way. That said, in this case as in most others, no single one-size-fits-all approach need govern the design and adoption of such frameworks

Indeed the legal and policy anchoring of evaluation can vary substantially across countries. Some countries have specific stipulations in their constitutions; others focus on primary or secondary law to anchor policy evaluation; while still others opt for flexible arrangements linked for instance to particular public-sector reform strategies.

Robust policy evaluation systems can benefit from clearly designated institutional actors with a well-defined mandate and specific resources to oversee and/or carry out policy evaluation. Here, the landscape is also quite diverse. While in some countries there is one, or a small number of organisation(s) promoting and/or coordinating policy evaluation across government, such a centralised element can also be absent, without necessarily precluding the existence of a strong evaluation culture.

Even if a clear central coordinating entity exists, it can be of a very different nature depending on the country:

- Some countries created departments or offices located within their CoG institutions (the Presidency, Cabinet Office, Government Office or Prime Minister Office).
- Other countries have established independent agencies that set and coordinate evaluations across government. Moreover, certain line ministries can also play a central role in promoting and/or co-ordinating policy evaluation across government.

What is evaluated might also affect the institutional set-up that is required. For instance, while independent bodies might be the best option for conducting or overseeing ex post evaluation of sensitive regulations with significant impact, line ministries and agencies in charge of the implementation of the evaluated policy might be more adequate to conduct less sensitive evaluations (OECD, 2018[52])

---

### Box 5.1. Canada's Policy on Results

In July 2016, the Government of Canada launched a Policy on Results, which seeks to improve the achievement of results across government and better understand the desired and obtained results and the resources used to achieve them.

Responsibilities on policy evaluation are shared between the Privy Council Office and the Treasury Board. These bodies are respectively responsible for promoting the use of evaluation findings into policy-making and defining and updating the evaluation policy.

The Policy establishes that all government departments should have an evaluation unit. On the other hand, Line Ministries are responsible for establishing a Departmental Results Framework. For the implementation of the policy, the Treasury Board of Canada can require departments to undertake specific evaluations and participate in centrally-led evaluations; initiate or undertake Resource Alignment Reviews; and approve Line Ministries Departmental Results Frameworks and changes to their organisations' core responsibilities.

Source: Treasury board of Canada Secretariat (2016[68]), Policy on results https://www.tbs-sct.gc.ca/pol/doc-eng.aspx?id=31300 (Accessed August 2nd 2019).

Supreme Audit Institutions can play a critical role in the evaluation process through their audits, evaluations and advice, thus holding the government to account for the use of public resources (see Box 5.2 for an example of Chile's Supreme Audit Institution's role in strengthening good governance). In addition to evaluating policies and programmes on a performance or value-for-money basis, SAIs can act as an "evaluator of evaluators" in government by auditing the effectiveness of an evaluation system and those responsible for it.

---

**Box 5.2. Chile's Supreme Audit Institution's role in strengthening good governance**

In 2014, the OECD conducted a Public Governance Review of the SAI of Chile. The Report finds that "Chile's supreme audit institution (Contraloría General de la República de Chile or CGR) is at the forefront of an evolution of Supreme Audit Institutions and has undertaken ambitious initiatives for institutional strengthening, capacity development, transparency and citizen participation. The CGR has introduced strategic planning, restructured its workforce and become an exemplary institution with respect to transparency within the Chilean public sector.

The CGR recognises its crucial role in contributing to good public governance, and has undertaken this OECD review to support ongoing initiatives, maximise the positive impact of its work on enhancing good public governance, and improve accountability and the quality of government decision-making. The CGR has the opportunity to further strengthen its solid reputation to position itself as a leader, providing objective and credible information that is widely recognised as useful for addressing challenges to good public governance. The review explores how the CGR's audit assignments could be adjusted to enhance the institution's impact on good public governance, and how it could further leverage knowledge gathered through existing and new audit assignments to deliver additional value to its diverse range of stakeholders.

Source: OECD (2014[69]), Chile's Supreme Audit Institutions: Engancing Strategic Agility and Public Trust, OECD Public Governance Reviews, OECD Publishing, Paris, https://dx.doi.org/10.1787/9789264207561-en.

---

### Promoting the quality and use of evaluations

Promoting policy evaluation across the policy cycle requires more than ticking the box that evaluations are produced. Ensuring the systematic production of policy evaluations is a necessary but insufficient condition to enhance the quality of public governance and service delivery. Poor quality evaluations will hardly contribute to better learning, higher accountability, or better decision-making and policy design, or better results for people. Likewise, high-quality evaluations may be completely ignored for actual policy decisions, due to a lack of incentives.

While the idea of fostering an evaluation culture can sound somewhat aspirational, concrete actions can be taken to promote the relevance and uptake of policy evaluations. These can for instance include the promotion of political commitment and stakeholder engagement (see chapter 1 and 2), or the support for skills development in the area of policy evaluation. Moreover, according to the *OECD The Path to Becoming a Data-Driven Public Sector Report*, fostering a Data Driven Public Sector culture can be a very effective way to enhance the quality of ongoing evaluations through the application of relevant data (OECD, 2019 [60]). Indeed, data in the public sector leads to an understanding of performance oriented towards an iterative approach to subsequent planning. Not only does an increase in the amount of data associated with policy outcomes allow for agile policy adjustments in the short-term, it can also generate better insights into the policy process in the mid- to long term. As a result, policymakers can assess whether policies have had the desired effect, and if that data is publish in Open Data format, so can other stakeholders. Policy evaluation can therefore become a more open, inclusive and ongoing process.

The **quality of policy evaluations** is an essential factor in guaranteeing the robustness and validity of any policy evaluation effort. Both quality control (deliverable oriented) and quality assurance (process oriented, i.e. doing the right things in the right way) are essential in this respect. For this reason, the *OECD Recommendation on Budgetary Governance* (2015[48]) [OECD/LEGAL/0410] recommends for instance that Adherents "ensure the availability of high-quality (i.e. relevant, consistent, comprehensive and comparable) performance and evaluation information to facilitate an evidence-based review".

An analysis of the data collected through the OECD Survey on Policy Evaluation shows that governments are focusing in enhancing skills and capacities within the public service to conduct or commission policy evaluations; and in promoting stakeholder engagement, to ensure that evaluations are targeted properly and that recommendations for improvement are practical and user-centred (OECD, 2018[67]) .

As shown in Figure 5.1, the **use of policy evaluation results in policy-making** represents an important challenge for governments in the area of policy evaluation[2]. Factors such as overall quality, timing of evaluations and political commitment to the evaluation process can increase the use (and therefore impact) of policy evaluation recommendations. Therefore, countries have developed specific initiatives to promote the strategic use of policy evaluation results. According to the results of the OECD Survey on Policy Evaluation, almost 50 % of surveyed countries (60%) for instance promote the use of policy evaluation through the incorporation of their findings in budgeting (OECD, 2018[67]). This aligns with the *OECD Recommendation on Budgetary Governance* [OECD/LEGAL/0410], which suggests that governments should take into account the results of evaluations to reassess the alignment of overall expenditure (including tax expenditure) with fiscal objectives and national priorities (OECD, 2015[48]) . More than one third of surveyed countries also foster the use of evaluations by discussing their results at the highest political level (Council of Ministries or equivalent). A similar number of countries has established co-ordination platforms to promote the use of evidence produced by policy evaluations.

According to the responses provided by countries to the OECD Survey on Policy Evaluation, countries are adopting different practices to fostering the use of evaluation results in policy-making:

- Norway has launched a web service (https://evalueringsportalen.no/), which gathers the findings of the evaluations carried out by the central government in one platform. By increasing accessibility to evaluation results, the Government aims to increase the use and reuse of knowledge and results from evaluations in all state policy areas, in future evaluations, and in society as a whole. It is moreover important for legitimacy and transparency in relation to government activities.

- The United States of America has created an Interagency Council on Evaluation Policy, co-chaired by the Office on Management and Budget (OMB) and the Department of Labor, composed of about ten high-capacity evaluation officers from government agencies, who meet on a monthly basis, to discuss evaluation results.

Moreover, in several countries evaluations results are discussed at the parliamentary level:

- In Germany, the Bundestag (the lower House of Parliament) requires annually approximately 80 reports from the Federal Government regarding the evaluation of single policies or specific regulations and measures of administrative action of the government. Over the past five years, the country has issued the following evaluation reports: Scientific Advisory Council of the Federal Government on Global Change (Wissenschaftlicher Beirat der Bunderegierung Globale Veränderungen); Main Report Monopolies Commission 2016 (Hauptgutachten Monopolkommission 2016); Evaluation of the Age Allowance Act (Evaluation des Altersgeldgesetzes).

- In Japan, the government submits a report each year to the Japan's bicameral legislature Diet on the status of Policy Evaluation and on how the results of such evaluation have been reflected in policy planning and development.

Source: (OECD, 2020[70]).

## Reviewing the impact of regulations

Evaluating regulations through *ex-post* regulatory reviews is primordial to ensure regulations in place are both relevant and adapted to their aims (OECD, 2017[1]). Following implementation, unintended consequences might emerge and need to be addressed. Alternatively, societal or technological changes may make a regulations obsolete. When *ex-post* regulatory reviews are not carried out, regulatory costs and red tape tend to incrementally increase, at the expense of businesses and citizens (OECD, 2017[1]). Ex-post reviews can therefore shed light on potential areas of improvement and therefore become a tool for regulatory planning.

The OECD Regulatory Policy Committee is discussing the development of Best Practice Principles for Ex Post Regulatory Reviews; based in the fact that despite their importance to improve the current regulation stocks and the design and administration of new regulations, they remain the less developed area of regulatory policy.

The document aims to provide general guidance in system governance, under the following overarching principles:

- Regulatory policy frameworks should explicitly and permanently incorporate *ex-post* reviews as an integral part of the regulatory cycle.
- A sound system for the *ex-post* review of regulation would ensure comprehensive coverage of the regulatory stock over time, while 'quality controlling' key reviews and monitoring the operations of the system as a whole.

Reviews should include an evidence-based assessment of the actual outcomes from regulations against their rationales and objectives, note any lessons and make recommendations to address any deficiencies. The Principles will address several governance dimensions, such as methodologies, public consultation and sequencing, capacity building and committed leadership for evaluations.

## Core questions for consideration

- Does your country's current legal and policy framework foster systematic policy evaluation across government? Are the necessary mechanisms in place to ensure ex-post evaluations of regulations?
- How does your government ensure the quality of evaluations across government? Are there specific mechanisms in place?
- To what extent does your government engage with stakeholders during the policy evaluation process?
- To what extent does your government provide a degree of transparency during the policy evaluation process?
- How does your government promote the use of the findings of policy evaluations? Does your government consider evaluation results for budgetary discussions? How is performance information use dot improve policy and service design and delivery? In other words, does your government institutionalise feedback loops to optimise the impact of the evaluation of policy performance and sustain its influence on policy-making?
- In the context of pursuing the Agenda 2030 SDGs, is policy evaluation and its feedback loops taking on added importance? How is your government preparing for assessing its progress in pursuing this Agenda and in reporting to citizens on this progress?
- Has your government established measures to promote the realisation of ex-post regulatory reviews?

## Additional resources

OECD legal instruments:

- Recommendation of the Council on Regulatory Policy and Governance (2012) [OECD/LEGAL/0390]
- Recommendation of the Council on Budgetary Governance (2015) [OECD/LEGAL/0410]

Other relevant OECD tools:

- OECD Improving Governance with Policy Evaluation: Lessons From Country Experiences (2020)
- OECD Best Practice Principles for Regulatory Policy: Reviewing the Stock of Regulation
- OECD Regulatory Policy Outlook (2018)
- OECD Performance Budgeting Survey (2016)
- OECD Supreme Audit Institutions and Good Governance (2016)

- OECD Framework for Regulatory Policy Evaluation (2014)

## References

Lázaro, B. (2015), Comparative study on the institutionalisation of evaluation in Europe and Latin America, Eurosocial. [66]

OECD (2020), Improving Governance with Policy Evaluation: Lessons From Country Experiences, OECD Public Governance Reviews, OECD Publishing, Paris, https://doi.org/10.1787/89b1577d-en. [70]

OECD (2019), The Path to Becoming a Data-Driven Public Sector, OECD Digital Government Studies, OECD Publishing, Paris, https://doi.org/10.1787/059814a7-en [60]

OECD (2019), Governance as an SDG Accelerator : Country Experiences and Tools, OECD Publishing, Paris, https://dx.doi.org/10.1787/0666b085-en. [47]

OECD (2018), OECD Regulatory Policy Outlook 2018, OECD Publishing, Paris, https://dx.doi.org/10.1787/9789264303072-en. [52]

OECD (2018), Survey on Policy Evaluation. [67]

OECD (2017), Government at a Glance 2017, OECD Publishing, Paris, https://dx.doi.org/10.1787/gov_glance-2017-en. [1]

OECD (2016), Open Government:The global context and the way forward, OECD Publishing, Paris. [23]

OECD (2014), Chile's Supreme Audit Institution: Enhancing Strategic Agility and Public Trust, OECD Public Governance Reviews, OECD Publishing, Paris, https://dx.doi.org/10.1787/9789264207561-en. [69]

OECD (2012), Recommendation of the Council on Regulatory Policy and Governance, http://www.oecd.org/regreform (accessed on 4 October 2019). [27]

Treasury Board of Canada Secretariat (2016), Policy on results. [68]

## Notes

[1] This definition is adapted from the Open Government: The global Context and the Way forward (OECD, 2016[23]), which is based on the "OECD DAC Glossary" in Guidelines for Project and Programme evaluation

[2] Chapter 2 of this Framework addresses the broader issues related to evidence-informed policy-making.